# What Lenders *Don't* Want You To Know

# What Lenders *Don't* Want You To Know

## How To Keep From Being Surreptitiously Ripped Off By Unscrupulous Mortgage Professionals

*Kevin Michael Melody*

Writer's Showcase
San Jose  New York  Lincoln  Shanghai

**What Lenders *Don't* Want You To Know**
**How To Keep From Being Surreptitiously Ripped Off**
**By Unscrupulous Mortgage Professionals**

Writer's Showcase
an imprint of iUniverse.com, Inc.

For information address:
iUniverse.com, Inc.
5220 S 16th, Ste. 200
Lincoln, NE 68512
www.iuniverse.com

This book is not meant to be a reference source for any specific mortgage
product or program. The product and program specific information stated
herein is, as of the date of its publishing, correct and current to the best of
the author's knowledge. However, no warranties are made, or intended to be
made, as to its actual correctness. The author advises readers to seek specific
program information from the appropriate sources.

ISBN: 0-595-18638-6

Printed in the United States of America

To my wife, Silvia, whose hearty laugh and boundless joie de vivre inspire me daily.

# Contents

# Epigraph

A promise unrealized is a promise never made.

# *Introduction*

A pretty receptionist greets you with a smile as you enter the office lobby—its walls crowded with department store art, corporate licenses, framed letters from satisfied customers—and seats you amidst plastic plants to await your turn. Phones ring, pagers beep, Muzak filters in and out. At length, you are escorted to the "signing" room—a cramped, windowless enclosure, not unlike the kind used by police to grill criminal suspects—and seated before a tiny wooden table, upon which awaits a stack of legal-sized paper crammed to the margins with fine print. Your loan officer enters with the "signer," handshakes and introductions are exchanged; then he leaves you alone with the stack, the signer, and your thoughts. The signer smiles and hands you a pen. You take it uncertainly and glance at the stack wondering: if all that text were removed and laid end to end, how far would it reach? Tokyo? Australia? A dull queasiness begins to rise in your stomach, calling to you like a distant foghorn; as if it were warning you of an impending collision with a large, unseen, floating object—*the closing costs!* You glance at your spouse—no help there—then back at the signer, who nods and smiles again, inclining his head toward the stack. You ask him if you can get the loan without having to sign all these papers. He chuckles politely and inclines his head again, urging you to proceed. You sigh and begin to sign.

If you've ever walked away from the signing table with the vague feeling of being had, or you tremble at the thought of even starting the process of buying or refinancing a home, you are suffering from a common malaise called *mortgagor's ignorance*. It is caused by an entirely reasonable fear of the unknown, particularly that which you cannot afford. This book is designed to shed the light of knowledge upon your ignorance, thereby freeing you from paralyzing anxiety or buyer's remorse and allowing you the confidence of knowledge. This book will *not* teach you how to get a *free* loan, because—despite what salespeople or advertisements may promise—there is *no such thing*. What it will do is show you is how to determine if what you're paying is fair and reasonable, and how to ensure that you'll actually get what you are promised.

# Part I

*Deciphering Mortgage Industry Jargon*

# *Caveat Emptor*

"Let the buyer beware" is a warning all consumers would do well to heed, especially when the product being purchased is complex and difficult to understand. This is particularly true of mortgages. For most people buying or refinancing a home, the details of a Truth In Lending disclosure statement may as well be written in Hieroglyphics. Borrowers often rely on the verbal explanations of a loan officer—who may, or *may not*, have their best interests in mind—simply because the charges associated with a mortgage loan *are* complicated and difficult to understand. Unfortunately, a home loan is generally the most expensive and *lengthy* financial commitment that most people will make in their lifetimes. Therefore, a lack of understanding as to how lenders charge for their services can have a costly, and long-term impact on a borrower's finances.

A mortgage transaction is also unique in the sense that one party (namely the lender, represented by a loan officer) can *unilaterally* change the terms *after* a deal has already been struck, and usually at a point where the other party has little power to argue. This is made possible by two things: first, that the transaction will not *close* for a considerable time after the deal is made; and second, that most consumers do not know how to verify what a loan officer promises them, nor how to compel him to make good on the promise. Therefore, in order to protect yourself against unscrupulous salespeople, and avoid paying much more than necessary (often without being aware of it!), or passing up savings that could have been yours simply by asking, it is critical to know *what* you're paying for, *how* you're being charged, and what constitutes a *fair* and *reasonable* charge. In order to reach that goal, you must first understand the meaning of the term "negotiable."

Superficially, the term "negotiable" seems to associate itself with some sort of bargain, but its actual definition (especially in the context of mortgage loans) is much closer to *unlimited*. The dictionary definition of "negotiate" is: to arrange or settle by discussion and mutual agreement. Therefore, a negotiable price is one that is not fixed at the outset, instead it is arrived at by a process of "discussion and mutual agreement." From the perspective of a purchaser (the borrower, in the case of a mortgage) negotiability of price represents an opportunity to acquire a desired item for *less* than he expected to pay. By contrast, the seller of such an item will likely have established the offering price somewhere *above* that at which he hopes to eventually sell it. Thus, the seller too hopes to settle the deal in his favor. When the two parties to such a transaction are relatively equal in terms of sales ability, product knowledge, and stake in the outcome, one may expect the transaction to be mutually beneficial. A good example would be that of a person who seeks to purchase a used vehicle from a private party (rather than a dealership). It's a relatively simple transaction involving moderate amounts of cash, very little time, and scant paperwork. Neither party is likely to be a professional salesperson, nor to have any special experience, skill, or training in automobile sales. Therefore, it is unlikely that a negotiable price will create the opportunity for one party to have a vast advantage over the other in this instance. By contrast, however, a mortgage transaction is quite a bit more complicated than that required to transfer ownership of a car. A simple *refinance* may involve as many as *eight* individuals or companies, each providing a separate—and necessary—service, in order to close. If your loan is for the *purchase* of a home, you'll probably need *twelve* or more. If you're depending upon the sale of your current home for the down payment of your new home (a "contingent" sale), just double that number; and that does not even count all the people incidental to the process—such as employers to verify income, landlords to verify rent history, lawyers to work out divorce settlements, and judges to rule on probate cases— just to name a few! The unique profile, circumstances, needs, and desires of each borrower, combined with the daily variability of mortgage rates, only make things even more complex. Couple that complexity with the fact that most people will buy only one or two houses in their entire lives; and that even if they refinance, or take out multiple loans on the same property, it is likely that years will separate the transactions (during which time market conditions change, loan programs come and go, regulations and required paperwork mount, and the necessity for specialized knowledge in order to make sense of it all increases); and it's not difficult to understand why most people have little idea as to how it all works. On the other hand, the individuals with whom one must deal in order to complete a mortgage transaction *are* professionals. They feed their families or starve based upon their ability to close loans on a *daily* basis. They maintain intimate contact with the vagaries of market conditions, regulatory changes, technology and product debuts. They continually educate themselves in sales techniques, and exercise their skills daily. In a transaction of this type, wherein the parties are so unequally matched, who do you think has the advantage when the cost is negotiable?

This is not to imply that all—or even *most*—mortgage professionals are amoral beasts, drooling at any opportunity to devour unsuspecting consumers. One's profession does not determine one's character. However, a wise consumer understands that even the best of us may submit to temptation from time to time, which brings me back to my theme.

The idea that you are on your own as a consumer, figuratively "swimming among sharks" is a fact of reality; but it is important to understand that the principle of Caveat Emptor *does not apply* to mortgage programs. In fact, it doesn't apply to rates, fees, terms, features, or even lending institutions. Caveat Emptor applies only to *individuals*—products don't cheat you, *people do*. Conversely, disclosure laws and regulatory authorities *do not protect you*; the former is meant to guide you in protecting yourself, and the latter is just there to devise the laws and help make you whole *after* you've been victimized. In fact, it is my experience that the more emphasis a borrower places upon getting the lowest quote on interest rate and loan costs (i.e., the product), as opposed to finding a mortgage professional who is not only skilled, but honest and ethical (i.e., the person), the more likely he is to end up accepting terms that are significantly different from those he expected to get. It is my opinion that the *person* with whom you ultimately choose to work is your best insurance of obtaining a reasonable deal. A salesperson who cannot sleep at night knowing he has done unto a client what he would never wish done unto him, will save you more money and grief than an entire encyclopedia of negotiating techniques and an Olympic stadium full of government regulators. I will demonstrate and emphasize that fact throughout this book.

# *Rate and Points:*
# *The Borrower's "Bubble"*

I have found that, in the realm of mortgage loan knowledge, most people float around in a bubble that contains the concepts "rate" and "points." Everyone seems to know what "rate" means in terms of what it will ultimately cost them, and most have heard the term "points," but only have a vague idea of its meaning. All the other costs and fees lay beyond the walls of the bubble; they can be seen by the borrower, but they're hazy, distorted, out of focus. This book is designed to burst that bubble, and the first step in that process is to clearly define the term "points."

I conduct consumer protection oriented home loan workshops on a regular basis, and one of the first things I do is ask if anyone in the crowd can define the term "points" as it relates to mortgage loans. I'm usually answered with blank stares, or wisecrack remarks like: "That's what I came here to find out!" Sometimes a brave soul or two will speak up with an uncertain quaver in his voice, saying something like: "Isn't that something you pay if you want a lower rate?" or: "I think that's one percent of the loan amount." One of my favorite responses is: "It's what you have to pay in order to get your loan closed!" In a certain sense all of them are partially correct.

The mistake most people make, if they have any sort of idea at all, is to assume that a "point" is some sort of fee. This could not be farther from the truth. The term "points" is simply mortgage industry jargon for *percentage* points. A percentage by itself cannot be a fee, because fees are paid in exchange for some sort of *service*. A percentage is a part of a larger whole; it is an *equation*. As it relates to mortgages, therefore, "points" are a means of calculating the dollar amount of a given fee, not fees in and of themselves. As a matter of fact, points will be used to determine the amounts of at least *four* different charges associated with a given transaction. But why, you may ask, don't we just call a duck a duck? Why quote an equation instead of the fee itself? The reason is simple, it's based upon a sales technique I call "reduction"; wherein a complex, industry specific pricing structure is "reduced," via jargon, to terms that are easier for a consumer to *think* he understands.

It's an embarrassingly obvious ploy once you realize how it works. Think about the term itself: this "." is a point. It's small; easy to chew, swallow, and digest; and *very* easy for a salesperson to *quote*. "That'll be 7.5% and 2 points, Ma'am." The idea is to get you thinking in terms of *small* things, and *pieces* of small things. The salesperson would much rather have you comparing fractions of differences in points between him and his competitors, than doing the actual calculation. Let's say, for example, you're requesting a $100,000 mortgage; those two points represent two *percent* of the loan amount, which means two *thousand* of your hard-earned dollars will now go flying out of your bank account! Imagine what it would be like if lenders quoted in terms of actual cost rather than percentages: "That'll be $7,500 per year for the next thirty years and $2,000 at the time of close, Ma'am." Have you ever in your life heard a salesperson speak in those terms? Of course you haven't! Because all his potential clients would be choking on their own spit and thinking twice about buying! The IRS has used this principle for decades to massive advantage; and as a result, most people I talk to, who receive a regular paycheck, have no clue whatsoever as to what they actually *pay* in taxes from each check. The IRS has trained them to focus on the net, and dangles a distractive carrot before them in the form of a refund at the end of the year. They are overjoyed if they get one, as if somehow this is not just a tiny portion of their own money coming back to them (without interest!), but rather some sort of unexpected windfall!

My point is this (no pun intended): in order to become a wise borrower you must train yourself to think in terms of *actual cost*; and in order to think in terms of actual cost, you must know how the calculations are made. With mortgage loans, many of the most costly fees are calculated as a percentage of the loan amount; and the jargon used to describe that percentage is the term "points."

# The "Origination" Fee:
# An Exercise In Semantics

I am continually surprised by the complete and utter silence I encounter when I ask my workshop groups for the definition of the term "origination" fee. I always take an informal survey before beginning, and generally find at least one or two individuals who have purchased multiple homes, rental properties, even commercial properties. Yet, among these allegedly experienced consumers, few have ever given me a satisfactory answer. Those who offer a response often pose it in the form of a question—as if they were guessing! Nonetheless, despite this common lack of knowledge, the concept is quite simple. The principle being applied here is plain old misdirection.

An "origination" fee is simply a euphemism for the lender's *commission*. I don't know the name of the marketing genius who came up with this term, but there is no doubt that he possessed a profound understanding of the human psyche as it relates to paying for things. The term "origination" has successfully taken the place of "commission" without assuming its commonly understood meaning of *payment for services rendered*. In other words, borrowers now seem to be under the impression that they are paying this fee as part of the cost of the money itself; when in reality, it is charged for the *service* of the provision of a loan. You pay the "originator" this fee for bringing you the money, the cost of money itself is a separate issue. The reason this works so well is that, for most people, it seems to be much easier to justify a $2,000 expenditure for the "purchase" of $100,000 of *money*—for example— than it is to pay the same amount for a salesperson to hand them an application to fill out, request copies of numerous personal documents, and sometimes return their phone calls! The truth is that you don't start "buying" the money you borrow until you begin making the monthly interest payments; and you'll continue to pay, and pay, and pay for that money for as long as the loan is outstanding. Aside from interest, every expense associated with a mortgage loan (which means most of the money due at closing) is paid in exchange for some *service* required to complete the transaction. Service is expensive (which is why most people are hesitant to call a plumber until there is an emergency, or a lawyer, until they are already in legal trouble); and in order to determine if its price is fair one must compare its cost to the price at which that same service could be purchased elsewhere.

Now, before we go further, it is essential that you thoroughly understand the two concepts we've covered so far: "points" are a means of *calculating* fees, and an "origination" fee is the lender's *commission*. Re-read everything up to this point if you must, but do *not* proceed until those two concepts are crystal clear in your mind; otherwise the information in this book will be useless to you.

Now that you've grasped the principles of cost of service versus cost of money, you must learn to distinguish the two from each other. I'll illustrate with the following example: Assume you wish to borrow $100,000 for the purchase of a home. Let's further assume that you've settled on a thirty-year loan at a fixed rate of 7.5% per year. If the loan is fully amortized (meaning it will be completely paid off at the end of the term), your monthly payment will be $699, most of which is interest (especially during the early years of the loan). In fact, after twelve months you will have paid $7,469 in interest, but your principle balance will have been reduced by only $922! Furthermore, if you keep the home for five years and make all the payments as per your contract, you will have paid and astounding $36,570 in interest, yet your loan balance will still be $94,618. In other words, after only one-*sixth* of the loan term has passed, the amount you have paid in interest alone is already equal to more than one-*third* of what you originally borrowed; yet you still owe almost *ninety-five percent* of the *original* loan amount, and you have another *twenty-five years* to go before it is paid off! But wait! That is only the cost of the *money*. You still haven't paid for the *service* of having the lender provide it for you. And if you agreed to an origination fee of only two tiny little points, you will have paid an *additional* $2,000 at the close of the loan, *before* you've even made your first payment, and we haven't even covered all the other fees yet! When presented in this context, does two "points" seem like a reasonable commission? The answer depends upon how much service you desire, or *require*, and what other providers are willing to accept in exchange for rendering the *same* service.

Here is where I want to make a very important point: you must understand that although the loan officer is nearly always splitting the commission with his employer (the lender or mortgage broker), the *amount* of the commission is generally determined by the loan officer himself. So, do not forget that Caveat Emptor applies only to *people*. Finding an honest, ethical loan officer is much more important than haggling back and forth over "points" in an attempt to reach an arbitrary figure that you deem acceptable; because, as will become clear, there are other, much less obvious ways that a loan officer can fatten his paycheck at your expense, *without* increasing the amount or quality of service you receive. (For more on the meaning of the term "service" see the chapter *Negotiating The Origination Fee*.)

Now, I know there are some of you out there thinking that you've already got this one figured out. The simple solution: a *zero points* loan! But why stop there? Why not go all the way and choose a zero *cost* loan? They certainly do exist. We hear them advertised all the time. Well, for those of you who have not yet begun to absorb the theme of this book, I'll pose another question. Do you think zero points means zero *commission*?

"Why not?" I hear you shouting. "They can take it out of all the interest they're going to charge me!"

That certainly would seem reasonable, if the lender were indeed going to *keep* all that interest. Yes, you read it right. The company that originally makes the loan to you is not going to benefit from receiving one dime of interest over the life of the loan, even if you choose a so-called "direct" lender; because nearly all of them will *sell* the residential loans they make within days of closing.

"But I've been making my payment to the same company for years!" you say.

No matter, the loan has more than likely been sold, and your lender has merely retained the right to collect the monthly payments and administer the loan on behalf of an investor who is the real owner of the mortgage. Furthermore, most lenders will not even make a loan in the first place unless they already have an investor waiting to purchase it. For those of you who thought there was some advantage to using a "direct" lender, all I can say is I'm sorry—there is no such thing.

I will explain how all this works in the next chapter. For now, just remember that unless your lender collects his profit at the close of the loan, he will have worked for nothing. Therefore, you will *always* pay a commission and other service fees at closing. Your only choice is that of the *form* in which they are paid (i.e., visible, or invisible). It will be your responsibility to determine *what* you are paying, and if it is reasonable. Here's a rule to help you decide on a fair price for services rendered: *Service can be good, fast, or cheap; but the best you can do is two out of three. You choose which two you want; the one leftover will be their price.*

# The Secondary Mortgage Market:
# The Money Behind The Money

The "Secondary Mortgage Market" is a generic term that collectively refers to all the various investors that purchase mortgage loans after they are closed. I mentioned earlier that nearly all residential mortgages will be sold immediately after closing, and that most lenders will not even make the loan in the first place unless they already have a buyer ready to purchase it. I also said that—even if you make your payment to the institution that originally lent you the money for the entire term of the loan—in all likelihood, they have only retained the right to collect the payment and pass it on to its true owner. I'll explain why they do this in a moment. First, a bit more about "direct" lenders.

In order to be a "direct" lender a company must have *its own money*. In other words, it cannot have borrowed the funds from any other source and assumed the obligation to pay them back with interest. This fact eliminates all banks, credit unions, savings and loans, mortgage bankers and mortgage brokers. In order to have money to lend, the first three must borrow from their depositors, or the Federal Reserve, or both. Mortgage bankers borrow their funds from banks; and Mortgage brokers merely act as middlemen between borrowers and lenders. A "direct" lender, therefore, is a myth. Once again some marketing mastermind has successfully convinced the general public to believe that if a company writes checks from its own accounts, it actually "owns" the money residing therein; and that this arrangement somehow confers upon the lucky company some sort of greater ability, or authority, by which they can beat out the competition.

The truth is that only an *investor* can be a "direct" lender in the sense that the advertising whiz kids would like you to believe banks are. This is because an investor really *does* own his money. He has no obligation to pay it back to anyone else. An investor, therefore, has a major advantage over "direct" lenders: he is beholden to no one but himself for the performance of his investments. If he chooses to gamble with risky borrowers, or lend his money out at interest rates that are well below the prevailing market, only *he* will reap the reward or suffer the loss. If the investor is a company, it is only slightly better off than a "direct" lender. If the company invests its clients' money poorly—and therefore loses it, or performs poorly in comparison to other investment companies—it will have trouble gaining and keeping clients, and will eventually go out of business. The main difference between an investment company and a bank, credit union, or mortgage banker, is that if it decides to invest in mortgages—and those mortgages go bad, or perform poorly—it has no obligation to make its clients whole.

So, there's no such thing as a "direct" lender. So, what? What does that have to do with the fact that lenders always sell their loans? It doesn't seem to make economic sense on the surface. After all, wouldn't they make a great deal more money by holding the loans and collecting interest over time? Well…yes! And they probably *would* hold all their loans if it weren't so risky for them to do so. Allow me to illustrate.

Let's say I'm "Bank Of The Cosmos" and I have branches all over the known universe. I control vast quantities of cash and throw it around in big chunks, treating it as if it were my own. I use a substantial amount of these funds to make mortgage loans to my customers and non-customers alike. Due to my great size, the principle of "economy of scale" allows me to offer interest rates that are better than any of my competitors. As a result, I make a tremendous number of loans, none of which I sell. Now, as long as most of the borrowers on these loans continue to make their payments, everything is fine. But what if something beyond my control happens? For example: What if the federal government raises income taxes and the economy takes a dive; Real Estate values drop and people start fleeing their over-encumbered houses in droves; a third of my outstanding mortgages go into default, and I find myself suddenly struggling to make ends meet. Meanwhile, the Federal Reserve chairman decides that the economy has been running a bit too fast and it's time to apply the brakes; so he tightens the money supply and raises the prime rate. Now in addition to having less income, my *expenses* have increased. I held onto my loans and just made interest payments to The Fed on the money I borrowed to make the loans in the first place (after all, it seemed like a good idea at the time; because the interest I earned on the loans I made was higher than what I had to pay on the money I had borrowed!); but now I have a big problem: the Fed can raise its rates any time it wants, and the new rate will apply to any money that I *currently* owe to them. Unfortunately, I will not be able to raise the rates my mortgage customers have agreed to; so now I'm being squeezed from two directions. What's worse, the higher Prime Rate spurs a series of increases in rates that other banks are willing to pay to their depositors; and as a result, I have to increase the interest rates I pay in order to keep my existing depositors from cashing out their accounts to put the money elsewhere. In a last ditch effort to save my business, I attempt to sell my portfolio of loans for cash. Unfortunately, the loans were made when interest rates were lower; therefore, in order to unload them I'll have to take a deep discount—which may make it difficult to cover the principle that I owe to the Fed. And what about the customers who are no longer making their payments? If I try to sell loans that are in default, I'll be lucky if I get pennies on the dollar! At this point, I have no choice but to declare bankruptcy.

The previous paragraph was a textbook description of how *not* to run a lending institution; and the same principles apply for *all* types of mortgage lenders since the money they lend is *borrowed* in the first place. It doesn't matter where they got it; what matters is that they have borrowed it on *short*-terms and at *variable* rates, and lent it out *long-term* at *fixed* rates (or at variable rates that cannot change as often, as quickly, or to such extremes as those at which they borrowed). Banks, savings and loans, credit unions, are all required to give their depositors their money *on demand*; therefore, they are extremely subject to market fluctuations of the type described above. If economic pressures shift and "Bank Of The Cosmos" cannot pay competitive rates to its depositors, they will take their money elsewhere; nevertheless the bank cannot demand its mortgage customers pay back all their loan principle whenever the bank needs it! The same thing applies to money borrowed from the Federal Reserve, and also to the terms under which banks lend money to mortgage bankers.

So, why do mortgage lenders make sure they have a ready, willing, and able buyer for all their loans before they make them? Because they don't even want to come *close* to finding themselves in the situation of "Bank Of The Cosmos." It is much safer for them to act as middlemen—who take their profit at the time the loan closes—and leave the risk-taking to investors. Nonetheless, you don't hear them shouting to the world about how it all works. This is because the marketing magicians have figured out that borrowers *like* "direct" lenders—and besides, why would *you* care anyway? Well, the answer to that question is what I am hoping to make clear to you. But we'll get into that a bit later. For now, just remember that mortgage lenders *don't* own the money they lend. Therefore, your loan *will* be sold, your lender will be earning his profit at the time of *closing* (on something other than interest), and you *will* be paying a commission and fees in one form or another. I will be helping you to figure out exactly how much you're paying, and how the lender is collecting it; it will be *your* job to determine whether that amount is fair in your case.

But before we get into that, for the sake of clarity, I must point out one more thing. In the last section, I stated that "…nearly all [lenders] will sell the residential loans they make…" The exception to that rule is called a "portfolio" lender—although, it is not a true exception, because these companies still borrow the money they lend from their depositors/clients, and still sell the loans the make into the secondary mortgage market. The difference is that they keep them for awhile first. Once they've become "seasoned" (usually after about two years or so, when the questionable borrowers have proven that they can and will pay back the debt), the loan becomes acceptable to the secondary mortgage market, and it is then sold. Portfolio lenders are the "Banks Of The Cosmos" in the real world; for the most part, they consist of small to medium sized companies that have a loyal clientele and a specific niche. The clientele may be depositors who wish to get a higher (albeit a bit more risky) return on their savings accounts; or the niche may be loans for commercial buildings, or unique properties, etc. Paradoxically, the most commonly known portfolio lenders (though, not nearly as numerous) are gigantic commercial banks or savings and loans. They can be easily identified by their above-market pricing, and their penchant for pushing variable rate loans (Washington Mutual would be a current example). There are advantages to using a portfolio lender if you are the type of borrower that is not easily categorized as "normal" (i.e., you're self-employed, have a marginal credit history, etc.), because the portfolio lender does not have to comply with secondary mortgage market underwriting guidelines. It must, however, cater to the higher cost of its clientele (depositors expecting higher rates on their savings/investment accounts). Therefore, the trade-off will *always* be higher cost to you—and usually the requirement that you accept a *variable rate* loan, which helps lower the risk for the lender of ending up like Bank Of The Cosmos. The Washington Mutuals of the world are becoming increasingly rare due to huge reserve requirements, higher default rates, and other factors that eliminate smaller companies from this niche; and a complete discussion of the pros and cons of using a portfolio lender is beyond the scope of this book. However, the principles I discuss herein are designed to arm you with the knowledge necessary to negotiate a reasonable and fair price for all costs involved with *any* mortgage transaction, regardless of the type of lender or loan product. So, remember, Caveat Emptor does not apply to institutions, programs, products, rates, and fees—*only to people.*

# *Lender and Third-Party Fees:*
## *"Go Forth And Multiply"*

We've talked about the commission; now let's talk about the other fees you will have to deal with. They come in two basic categories: those that are charged by the *lender*, and those that are charged by various *third parties*; but regardless of who is charging them, they are *all service fees*. Do you remember that I said you will be dealing with at least eight separate people on even the simplest of mortgage transactions (a refinance); and that if you're purchasing a property it may be twelve or more? Let's list some examples of third parties. The first one that comes to mind is the credit reporting company—you'll have to have a credit check—and although the lender collects the fee, a separate company runs your credit. You will also have to have the property appraised and inspected; you'll need a neutral third party to handle all the legal papers (escrow), and another to insure the title; then there's the possibility of a termite report; and, of course, we'll have to record the note. But that's not all! If a mortgage is being paid off as a part of the transaction, you may have to pay demand, reconveyance, and wire transfer fees, and possibly a sub-escrow to handle it; and don't leave out the guy who will have to shuffle all that documentation between locations in a hurry in order to meet one of many deadlines (messenger fee). Let's put them in table form for clarity:

| Credit | Appraisal | Inspection |
|---|---|---|
| Escrow | Title Insurance | Termite Report |
| Recording | Demand | Reconveyance |
| Wire Transfer | Sub-Escrow | Messenger |

The above list does *not* include any ongoing expenses that are prorated at close and continue to be charged throughout the life of the loan. We refer to such ongoing expenses as "recurring" costs; and they comprise interest on the loan itself, property taxes, hazard insurance, and—depending upon the amount of down payment or equity— mortgage insurance. I will not be discussing "recurring" costs because our primary concern is "non-recurring" charges—in other words, only those items that you pay once, at close, and never again as long as you hold the loan. It is the non-recurring charges that are the most likely to be negotiable (since they are all service fees, and therefore subject to Caveat Emptor), which means they are the most likely to end up costing you more if you don't pay attention.

Now, we've provided some examples of third party fees, but what about the lender fees? Let's list some examples: First things first: we may have to charge you an application fee; because our pricing is so low, and our service so great, that customers are lining up outside our doors hoping to do business with us; and we don't want to waste our time with you if you're not serious. Next, we have to have someone process the paperwork, an underwriter to make the yes-or-no decision on your loan, yet another person who will prepare the loan documents, and of course, someone to write the check and fund the loan. Meanwhile, we have to pay someone to watch over all these people—we'll call him the administrator, and someone else to bring them all coffee—we'll call him the researcher; and during the time your loan is in process, we'll certainly have to keep the money *somewhere*, so we'll just store it in our "warehouse." And let's not forget that we must pay the creative genius who comes up with the names and explanations for all these fees! Her name is Ms. Cellaneous. Okay, what've we got?

| Application | Document Preparation | Research |
|---|---|---|
| Processing | Funding | Warehousing |
| Underwriting | Administration | Miscellaneous |

Are you starting to get the picture? The point is this: there is no limit to the amount or type of fees that you may be charged. We lenders are only limited by our imaginations and your willingness to pay. (And believe me, any loan officer worth his salt as a sales professional will have a portfolio of ready-made, well-rehearsed, and quite convincing explanations to justify *any* fee.) There is no law that places a cap on these things—except, of course, the law of the jungle. But since this book is educational in nature, we'll refer to that law by its Latin terms:  Caveat Emptor. Are these fees negotiable? Of course! Everything is negotiable. The real question is: will *you* be successful in negotiating them in *your* favor? In *Part III*, I'll show you some ways that you can keep the "balance of power" on your side, but first let's define it.

# The Balance Of Power:
# To Know It Is To Love It

What is meant by the "Balance Of Power"? Put simply, it refers to the relative strength or weakness of either side in any negotiation. By strength, I am referring to an individual's ability to turn the negotiation to his favor; weakness, of course, refers to the opposite. Do you remember my example of buying a used car from a private party? That is a good illustration of a negotiation wherein the negotiating power is relatively balanced. On the other hand, nearly any *mortgage* transaction is likely to be heavily weighted in favor of the salesperson. However, that is not the case at the very beginning of the negotiation.

There are two things I want to you inscribe in letters of fire upon your brain right now. Put them right next to the principle of Caveat Emptor applying only to people! First, that you, as a consumer, have the ultimate power in any mortgage transaction, which is the power to withdraw and find another lender, or just decline to get a loan at all. (There is even a bit of actual law on the books that works in your favor here.) Second, the moment you decide to commit yourself to a lender by applying with him, that power begins to slide over to the lender's side; and the closer you are to the actual close of escrow, the less likely you will want to—or be able to—exercise your power to walk away. I will illustrate how this works in the next section; for now, just remember the principle: *you* have the power at the *beginning*, your *lender* has it towards the *end*.

# The "Discount": How To Pay More For Less

What is a "discount" as it pertains to a mortgage transaction? In my workshops, the usual response to this question is complete silence. By this point, even the experienced borrowers are beginning to question their own knowledge and abilities, so I generally give them a hint. What does it sound like it is *supposed* to be doing for you? Now I get all kinds of wisecrack replies from the burgeoning cynics in the crowd, the most common of which is: "It sounds like it should be lowering something, but I doubt that it will benefit me!" Well, the first part is correct: paying a discount buys you a lower interest rate. Whether or not it will actually be to your benefit will depend greatly upon whom you ultimately choose as your loan officer.

So, how does it work? We've learned that the term "points" does not refer to any specific fee, but rather to a means of calculating fees; and that the origination fee (commission) is calculated using points. Here they will be employed yet again to figure the discount. Yes, it is a percentage of the loan amount; but remember, your loan officer probably won't break down the points for you. You'll receive a quote that includes a rate, and one number referring to the points, such as: "That'll be 7.5% and 2 points." What you won't hear is: "That'll be 7.5% and 2 points, both of which will be my commission, and neither of which will be used to discount your rate." It is done this way in order to make the quote easier for you to swallow… Er…I mean, understand (or *think* you understand, anyway!).

What you're supposed to be getting in exchange for this additional money is an *interest rate* that is *lower* than the prevailing rates. The "prevailing" rates, in laymen's terms, are those that are most commonly advertised/quoted on any given day. Precisely defined, they are the rates at which a given investor will pay full face value for a given mortgage loan on a given day. Got that? I didn't think so. Okay, let me explain…

First, understand that the portion of the points that will go towards the *origination fee* is somewhat subjective. Since you're paying for *service*, the amount will depend upon what competitors are willing to accept in exchange for the same service (provided, of course, that you actually shop around!). On the other hand, the points you pay for a *discount* are an objectively determined, direct benefit to you (or *should* be, anyway). In an ideal world, you agree upon a given amount for commission; and if you want to discount your rate, the amount that it costs the lender to obtain the discount should be the exact additional amount you are charged. In other words, your desire (or need) to secure an interest rate that is below the prevailing rates should not be an excuse for the lender to raise his commission without your knowledge! The problem you face as the borrower is that you do not know what the lender's wholesale cost is for a given discount; and since most borrowers have no idea how this all works, they have no frame of reference under which to judge the cost. Thus, it is rarely questioned.

You may be thinking to yourself: "Why would I want a discount anyway?" Well, there are any number of reasons. You may have a budget consideration that is not quite in line with the current market conditions. In other words, you want your payment to be X dollars per month or less; but current interest rates are a bit too high to make that happen. Or maybe you're purchasing a property from a motivated seller who is willing to pay a nice chunk of your closing costs. If the amount he is willing to pay exceeds your actual costs, or you already have enough cash to cover them, why let it go to waste? You might as well let the seller buy you a permanently lower rate. Here is one that I see quite often: a "conditional" approval, which means that your loan has been approved with the condition that you are able to get a certain interest rate. If prevailing rates are higher, you'll have to pay for a discount. This is quite common because people are often trying to qualify for loan amounts that they can just barely afford; and there are many valid reasons for being in that situation. In my experience, people buying a new home will nearly always try to find the best home they can possibly afford at any given time. This is true for first-time buyers as well as those upgrading to more expensive homes. After all, a more expensive home generally means a better neighborhood and higher quality construction; both of which can mean greater appreciation in value over time, and less maintenance costs; not to mention the fact that you'll be less likely to want to move if you're satisfied with the neighborhood and the property. On the other hand, a refinance often involves cash out that is intended to consolidate other debts, or pay for home improvements, a college education, or the purchase of a big-ticket item such as a recreational vehicle or a boat—things that can be (or become) necessities, the acquisition of which may distract a borrower's focus from the cost of the loan. In either case, a borrower may find himself pushing the limits of what he is able to afford as far as a monthly payment. Combine that with fluctuating interest rates and you have the recipe for a conditional approval. The reason, however, isn't as important as the cost. So how do you find out what it will cost? I don't hear you answering! If you had no clue as to how to find out, whom would you think to ask? That's right! You'd ask you're friendly, knowledgeable, experienced, skilled, personable, honest, and ethical loan officer; and he'll be more than happy to give you a new quote. But where does your loan officer get *his* information? And how do you determine if the cost he quotes you is fair? The answer to both questions can be obtained in the secondary mortgage market.

Remember, all lenders will be selling the mortgages they make; and the "secondary mortgage market" consists of investors. They are usually large companies with enormous piles of cash that they need to invest on behalf of their clients. Two of the biggest are quasi-governmental organizations by the names of the Federal National Mortgage Association (Fannie Mae), and the Federal Home Loan Mortgage Corporation (Freddie Mac). Other examples include mutual funds, insurance companies, pension funds, government and municipal bond programs, etc. It is they who are really calling the shots in the mortgage industry by establishing guidelines under which they will buy mortgages, and thereby defining the types of products that lenders are willing to offer, and the rules under which borrowers will be qualified. Secondary mortgage market investors also determine what price they will pay for a given mortgage on a given date; and their pricing is determined by many of the same factors that drive other aspects of the economy. A discussion of those factors is not necessary for our purposes here; it will suffice that you understand that the big guys behind the scenes are—for the most part—making all the rules.

Now, what are the mechanics involved? Figure 1 is a simplified representation of a lender's wholesale rate sheet. The left hand column shows a graduated scale of interest rates; and the right hand column shows the discount cost (in "points") at the corresponding rate—but this is the *lender's* cost, not yours; and he must *add* to it his commission. Note that as the *rate* goes down, the *cost* goes up. At the top, there is a zero in the cost column, which signifies the prevailing or "par" rate for this investor on this date. This is the rate at which the investor will pay *full face value* for a closed loan. Thus, in this example, if you get a $100,000 mortgage at 7.5%, your lender will be able to sell the note for $100,000. His profit will then be any commissions and fees that he has charged you at close. On the other hand, if the lender writes the loan for a *lower* rate, then he will have to sell it for some figure *below* $100,000 (which is called "discounting" the note); because investors are not in a hurry to invest their money at anything less then the *maximum* possible yield. The same $100,000 loan, therefore, at a rate of 7.0%, would be discounted by 1.5% to $98,500. Since the amount of the note is $100,000, your lender will have to collect the difference from you. The lender's cost, therefore, should be "passed through" to you in exchange for the lower rate. In other words, unlike the points charged for an origination fee—which is paid in exchange for *service*—discount points are a part of the cost of the *money* (i.e., they are paid in exchange for *product*), and as such, *should* be a "pass-through" cost. What they should *not* be is a means by which your loan officer can increase his commission without your knowledge or consent! Let me give you an example of what to watch out for.

| FIGURE 1 | | |
|----------|------|---|
| Rate | Cost | |
| 7.500 | 0.000 | Prevailing Rate (Par) |
| 7.375 | 0.375 | |
| 7.250 | 0.750 | |
| 7.125 | 1.125 | |
| 7.000 | 1.500 | |

For the purposes of this illustration, I will introduce you to Don and Donna Jumbo. Mr. and Mrs. Jumbo are first-time buyers seeking a home in Orange County California. They are recently married, both professionals, and plan on starting a family soon. They've entered into a contract to purchase a nice home in a nice neighborhood with nice schools and nice neighbors. Very nice, indeed... The person who is arranging their loan is Mrs. Jumbo's sister's husband's brother's best friend's uncle's son, who happens to be a loan broker. Because of the close family relationship, they are certain to get a *great* deal! For the purposes of this example, we'll jump in after the loan has already been approved; and the Jumbos are now scheduled to close in a little over a week. Their loan officer has just called them up to tell them that all outstanding requirements have been met and he is now ready to request the loan documents. However, there is a slight problem: the Jumbos loan approval has been conditioned upon a rate of 7.25% or better. Today, however, the prevailing rates are at 7.5%. Don and Donna must now decide whether pay for a discount or cancel the transaction.

Remember the "Balance Of Power"? Let's analyze the situation and see exactly where it lies now. Mrs. Jumbo has already measured every room in the house and decided what furniture will go where and even ordered some new pieces to fill the empty spaces. She's decided on the color of the carpeting, style of drapes, and of course, all new towels, sheets, blankets, etc., to match the new décor. Mr. Jumbo already knows where all of his tools will be placed in their new two-car garage, and exactly how he wants the landscaping; he's been to Barbecue Bonanza a number of times and has his eye on a beautiful new gas grill for the patio. They have given notice at the place they currently rent, sent out change-of-address forms to all their creditors, subscriptions, etc., and invited everyone they know to a housewarming party two weeks from now. In their minds, the Jumbos have already moved into their new dream home; but their commitment is not merely emotional—because they put up a good faith deposit at the start of escrow; and since their loan has been approved, they are now *legally obligated* to complete the purchase or forfeit the deposit to the seller. If they don't like the quote their loan officer now gives them, what is the likelihood that the market conditions will remain unchanged long enough for them to bail out, start all over again with another lender, get *better* terms—and still close in a week? Not bloody likely at all! It seems, therefore, that the balance of power has shifted almost entirely onto the loan officer's side. In reality, the Jumbos can still walk away; but in my ten years in the mortgage profession, I have *never* seen it happen. The Jumbos are now totally dependent upon their loan officer to make their dream home a reality. They are likely to do whatever he advises and—trust me—he is not unaware of this fact! It is here that temptation may rear its ugly head and sorely test his mettle; but don't blame the program or the economy or the circumstances for what may happen next—Caveat Emptor does *not* apply to them!

So, what do the Jumbos do? First, they'll ask how much it will cost, at which point the loan officer will check his wholesale rate sheets. Referring back to Figure 1, we see that in order to lower the rate from 7.5% to 7.25%, the lender's cost will increase by 0.75% (¾ of a point). Don and Donna negotiated a 1.375% commission with their loan officer; and he will now have to do a bit of math in order to come back to them with the proper figure. Why don't we peek inside his head and check his addition?

"Hmmm… Let me see… a 1.375% commission, plus a 0.75% discount, equals a total of 2.375%, correct? Wait a minute! Something's wrong here! Let me add that again: 1.375 plus 0.75 equals 2.5, right? No? How about 2.625? 2.875? Darn, I always have the toughest time adding fractions. Well, I guess I better be safe and just round up!"

Are you starting to understand the process here? The fact that Don and Donna Jumbo will never, *ever* see his wholesale rate sheet—and therefore will never *know* what his actual discount cost is—has had a debilitating effect upon Mr. Loan Officer's capacity to add. When they hear the final quote, the Jumbos will swallow hard and be silent for a few moments; then they'll ask their loan officer if there is any way to close the loan for less money. (It bears mentioning that the loan officer is by now intimately familiar with the Jumbos financial resources; thus he knows exactly where the breaking point lies as far as affordability is concerned.) He'll shake his head slowly, and with a solemnly sympathetic expression say: "I'm really sorry, but that's the cost of the discount, I'm just passing it through to you." There will be another few seconds of silence; then the Jumbos will say: "Okay. When do we come in to sign the documents?"

Yes, I can hear you screaming: "I would never agree to that!"

Well of course you wouldn't, not after having it presented to you from the *loan officer's* perspective! Don and Donna did not have that advantage. But let's just suppose—for the sake of argument—that Mr. Loan Officer is incapable of telling a falsehood. Yet, this handicap has not had any effect upon certain *other* aspects of his character. In that case his quote might sound something like this:

"You guys are in luck today! I can get you the discount you need. My cost on that will be a mere ¾ of a point. Now, I know we agreed upon a 1.375% commission; but since I'm saving your deal for you, I believe I'm entitled to a reward. So, I'm going to go ahead and raise my commission to 1.75% and add my discount cost on top. Is that all right with you?"

Do you think the Jumbos would agree to pay if it were presented that way? Not only no, but h—-no! Which is exactly why it *won't* be presented that way.

"But Kevin, how do you expect us to fight against something we don't know is happening? What do we do?"

Have patience, my friends. I promise not to leave you unarmed in this fray; but we still have some ground to cover before we get to that.

# "Overage":
# The Invisible Fee

At the beginning of every one of my workshops, I always ask the attendees to raise a hand if they have ever purchased a home before; and on average, about half the crowd does so. I then ask if anyone has purchased more than one home or property; and most of the hands go down. I continue with: "Who's done it more than twice?" "More than three times?" "Four?" and so on. The lucky person who holds his hand up the longest gets the privilege of trying to answer the next question: What is an overage?

I've been doing home loan workshops since 1997, and I have never once gotten a satisfactory answer. Most people just shrug their shoulders and say something like: "I have no idea whatsoever; but from what I've learned so far, I bet it's going to cost me something."

Yep. It will.

Do you remember the "zero points" loan? Well, it isn't a zero *commission* loan, any more than a zero cost loan is *free* money! The costs have not gone away, they have simply changed form; and an overage is the mysterious and magical process by which they have been rendered invisible.

To understand how this works we have to integrate two concepts we've already discussed. Our old friend "points" will be used once more for the calculations; and we will need to take another look at the lender's wholesale rate sheet. Do you remember the simplified representation in Figure 1? Well, it was simplified by exactly half. Figure 2 shows the whole thing.

| FIGURE 2 | | |
|---|---|---|
| Rate | Cost | |
| 8.000 | -2.000 | |
| 7.875 | -1.500 | |
| 7.750 | -1.000 | |
| 7.625 | -0.500 | |
| 7.500 | 0.000 | Prevailing Rate |
| 7.375 | 0.375 | |
| 7.250 | 0.750 | |
| 7.125 | 1.125 | |
| 7.000 | 1.500 | |

As you can see, the prevailing rate does not represent the *top* of the market, but rather its *middle*; and in the same manner that the lender's cost increases as the rate drops below market, it *decreases* for rates above it—all the way into *negative* numbers. What this literally means is that a loan closed with an above-market interest rate can be sold for *more* than its full face value. Using Figure 2 as an example: if you got a loan for $100,000 and agreed to a rate of 7.875%, the lender would be able to sell the note for $101,500 ($100,000 x 1.5% = $1,500). The investor is willing to pay more because the note will generate a greater return than one at the prevailing market rates. Therefore, the trade-off for lower costs is *always* a higher rate (and sometimes the addition of a pre- payment penalty on top!).

Yes, I hear you're exasperated cry: "Kevin! Why would I agree to accept a higher rate?"

You'd do it because it would *benefit* you to do so. For example: maybe you're in the opposite situation of Mr. and Mrs. Jumbo; you have no problem qualifying for the loan income-wise, but your savings account is being severely strained trying to come up with enough cash at close. In that case, a few extra dollars on the monthly payment may be a reasonable exchange for the benefit of low or no closing costs. Or perhaps you're refinancing in order to combine existing first and second mortgages into one loan at a lower rate, but you have a problem with equity. If you increase the loan amount to include closing costs, your proposed loan will exceed the loan-to-value[1] (LTV) limits of the program you want. In this case, accepting a slightly higher rate in exchange for reduced or eliminated costs may be preferable to paying them out-of-pocket. Another classic example is that of the individual who has a mortgage at a rate that is significantly above the market (perhaps he had credit problems, or some other issue at the time the existing loan was made); and he wishes to refinance to lower it, but does not intend to stay in the property for more than a year or two after the loan closes. He may well be able to lower his rate significantly and still be enough above the market to get a zero cost loan. If so, he won't have to raise the loan amount to cover costs (and thus reduce equity), or pay them out of pocket. He gets a significantly lower payment for the next couple years, and he is unlikely to pay as much in additional interest as he would have paid in total closing costs had he taken market rates. As you can see, it is not a matter of zero points and zero cost programs being inherently evil. Just like everything else we've talked about, you need to determine if the benefit is worth the price. So, how do you figure that out? Well, *that's* the problem, because there is no law that requires lenders to *disclose* the amount of an overage. In other words,

---

1. Loan-to-value or "LTV" is the ratio between the combined balances of all mortgages on the property and its actual present value. For example: a loan of $75,000 on a property worth $100,000 is at 75% LTV, meaning 75% of the value of the property is encumbered by loans. All loan programs have some maximum LTV; and as a general rule, the better the rate and terms of the loan, the lower the acceptable LTV.

allowing a lender to use an overage to pay your costs effectively gives him permission to charge whatever he wants, without having tell you the actual amount.

Let me see if I can make this a little clearer. Let's say you negotiate a 1% commission with your lender. He then presents you with the option to pay no "points" in exchange for a slightly higher rate. It might go something like this: "I can give you 7.5% for 1 point. Or 7.875% for no points." He will then proceed to give you an "objective" overview of the pros and cons of each option as it applies to your particular circumstance, in order to "help" you decide. His pitch will be smooth and polished; and when he's done, he'll ask you to choose one or the other. Let's assume he's using the rate sheet in Figure 2 for his quote. If you choose 7.5% he'll have to disclose his commission, and must therefore keep it reasonable; but if you choose the "no points" option at 7.875%, he'll earn a half-point more—and he *won't* have to tell you how much he's made. To you it will appear as if he's working for free! Given the fact that he is a professional salesperson—who is paid by commission, which option do you think will sound more attractive to you after he's done with his pitch? If you knew what your loan officer knew, you'd understand that his well-rehearsed pitch really boils down to a simple alternative: "Mr. Borrower, Sir. Would you like to pay me 1% for my services or 1.5%? The type and quality of service you receive will remain the same in either case; but I'll be much happier if you choose the latter." If your loan officer made his pitch that way, would you agree to pay him the higher amount? Probably not. That's why it *won't* be presented to you that way. As with all the other things we've covered so far, I'll show you how to make sure you're not over-paying for overage pricing in *Part III*. Also, please pay special attention to this item if you are considering an FHA or VA loan (see *Special Programs* in *Part V* for specific things to watch out for on government loans). And now, on to the last item!

# The "Lock":
# An Unsung Hero

Strangely, enough, many people I teach in my workshops know exactly what a "rate lock" is; what they don't know is what it *costs,* and what it *really* does for them. In its simplest terms, a "lock" fee is a charge you pay to guarantee that you'll get a specific interest rate when your loan closes. If you choose not to pay for a lock, then the rate you get is subject to whatever the prevailing rates are at the time your loan documents are prepared. Why does that matter? It matters because market conditions—and therefore, rates—change *daily*; and most transactions require thirty days or more to close. Without a lock, you may end up having to accept an interest rate that is higher than what you expected by the time you're ready to close. On the other hand, rates may be the same, or maybe even lower! How do you decide if you should lock or take a calculated risk? Well, first you'll have to know how to do the calculation; and I'll give you one guess as to how we figure the cost! Yes, you're right! We use "points."

The cost of a rate lock will vary according to prevailing market conditions and the amount of time you need. The fee actually goes to the investor who will ultimately buy your loan, in exchange for setting aside the money that will be used to purchase your loan, during the time period requested. For example: to guarantee a rate for thirty days under normal market conditions will probably cost you approximately 0.25% (¼ point). This amount is, like all the others, added into the total; and you will be quoted one number that includes *all* the various fees calculated using points. To get forty-five days you should expect to pay about 0.5% (½ point), and sixty days may cost you 0.75% (¾ points) or more (see Figure 3).

| FIGURE 3 | | |
|---|---|---|
| 30 days | 45 days | 60 days |
| 0.250 | 0.500 | 0.750 – 1.000 or more |

Now, if you've ever done a mortgage transaction before, my question to you would be: did you request a rate lock at the time you applied for the loan? If you're like most people, you did not. There are two compelling reasons for this. First, most people have at least a modicum of prudence when it comes to spending their money—provided, of course, that they *know* they are spending it! Let's take the example of the $100,000 mortgage (those of you in Orange County and Beverly Hills will have to do the appropriate multiplication), a lock for which could cost you anywhere from $250 (0.25% x 100,000 = 250) up to as much as $750 or more, depending on the amount of time you need. What will you receive in return for your money? You'll get about a month or so of rate "insurance." We all know how insurance works, right? It only pays off if the "bad" thing happens, which in this case means rates have risen. If you have a lock, and rates go up, you'll easily save much more in interest over time than the cost of the lock. But what if rates don't change? Will you get your money back? Nope. I don't know of any insurance company that returns premiums to customers who don't make claims! How about if rates go down? Correct! We keep your money in that case also.

"But, Kevin," I hear you say—and I can picture the hopeful expression on your face, "if I have to give up the cost of the lock, will I at least get the lower rate?"

Sorry, no.

You see, when you ask your friendly loan officer to lock your rate for you, he will have to ask his *investor* to reserve the money for you. The investor must then refrain from investing that money elsewhere during the lock period, hence, the cost. Furthermore, that investor will be expecting to buy the loan at the guaranteed rate at the end of the lock period—it's as much a guarantee for the investor as it is for you! If rates drop during the lock period and your lender gives you the lower rate, he will now have to pay discount points to the investor when he sells the loan—probably wiping out any profit he's made. Which fact brings us to the second reason most people don't lock at the time of application: their loan officer never brings up the subject. And why should he? If you lock, and rates drop significantly before your loan closes, your lender will not be able to offer you the lower rate without charging you additional money; which means that he will probably have to watch you go to a competitor. Thus, you have two forces working against the likelihood of a lock. First, there's your own sense of financial prudence (who wants to spend hundreds of dollars that may either go to waste or actually work against you?), then there's the loan officer's desire to increase his chances of actually earning a commission (what commissioned salesperson would ever voluntarily place himself in a situation that may end up forcing him to give up a good client?). The result: people rarely request a lock at the time of application.

Okay, now that I've said all that, I want to encourage each one of you to *please lock* your interest rate *at the time you apply* for your next loan!

"What!" you scream. "But, you just told me that locking didn't make financial sense!"

No, not exactly. I explained how a lock fee is *calculated*, and why most people *don't* lock; but the truth is, in nearly every case, a lock is one of the absolute best things you can do for yourself. One of the most important reasons for this is that lenders only advertise—and loan officers only quote—*short*-term rates.

What is a short-term rate? I'm glad you asked! The most exact definition is: the rate at which a given investor will *not* charge a lock fee; and the only time an investor is willing to do that is when the lender can guarantee that the loan will be delivered—lock, stock, and barrel—in a relatively short time frame. That time frame can be as little as five days, but never more than 15 days. (Those are *calendar* days, by the way, which means only five to ten *business* days.) And if you've ever gone through the process of application, approval, conditions, documentation, funding and closing involved in even the simplest of mortgage transactions, you understand that ten business days is rarely time enough. On the other hand, if you've already applied, had your credit checked, supplied any required documentation, been approved, provided any conditions required prior to closing, and are ready to draw up the documents, that's a different story! At that point, there is not much standing in the way of closing, and the lender can be fairly certain he'll be able to meet such a short deadline, which is exactly why most loan officers will not encourage you to lock until they have brought you to that point. They will, however, not be at all hesitant to quote you a rate that does not include a lock fee, and therefore sounds lower.

Why is a low quote so important? In my experience, there are three things that people are comparing when they shop for a mortgage loan: rate, fees, and service. Of those three which do you think carries the most weight with the average borrower when he is making his final choice? I'm sure I don't have to tell you that it is the rate. And you are right to be concerned. After all, you'll only be paying the closing costs one time; you'll only experience your loan officer's wonderful service for about a month or so; but you'll be paying that interest rate for the next fifteen to thirty *years*. You'll be reminded of it every time you sit down to write out a check to your lender; and over time, even a small difference in rate can add up to a large amount in actual dollars paid.

Now, I know of no loan officer who is ignorant of the fact that most consumers are extremely rate conscious. They are also quite familiar with what happens if a potential client doesn't get a quote that is lower than the best one he's heard that day: the depressing sound of a dial tone. He knows that if the potential customer doesn't hear what he wants to hear, the loan officer will never get a chance to sit down with him and give him his best sales pitch. Therefore, he must give the lowest quote he can honestly give (or that which he honestly thinks he can get you to believe). Nevertheless, the truth is that a quote is just a conglomeration of air molecules massaging your eardrums and numbing your financial sensibilities; it means nothing unless the loan officer can actually *deliver* what he promised within the time required to close your loan. In my opinion, it is dishonest (and dishonorable) for a loan officer to quote a rate without including the time frame for which it is good, because most borrowers will assume that they can actually get that rate. Therefore, if you rely upon quoted rates as the most heavily weighted factor in your decision of what lender to use, you are virtually guaranteed *not* to get what you were promised.

My goodness! Is there nothing to be done? Read on, my friend. All will be made clear soon...

# Part II

*Preparation—A Three Step Program*

# *Step 1: Do Unto Others...*

I've spent the majority of this book so far trying to hammer home the concept that the time you take choosing a loan officer is orders of magnitude more important than that which you spend shopping lenders, programs, rates and fees. This is because a good loan officer will act as your advocate—rather than your adversary—in this complex, and lengthy transaction. He will put himself in your shoes and work as if every penny spent were his own, and he knows more about the inner workings of the industry than you could ever hope to learn in a month or two. Having a person like that, an insider, as your champion and guide will pay off in big savings and invaluable peace of mind. Therefore, you must <u>find the most honest</u> and <u>ethical person</u> you possibly can; you want the kind of person that cannot live with himself if he thinks that he has cost you one dime more than he would have charged his own mother, or that you've received anything less than perfect service—but how do you find such a person?

The first step in your search is to understand, and accept, the Golden Rule. In the realm of capitalism, "do unto others..." translates to "you get what you pay for." You cannot expect honesty and fairness from those with whom you wish to do business, if you are not prepared to offer it yourself. Do not expect to receive comprehensive, detailed, and accurate information unless you are ready to provide it on your part. If you make yourself accessible, return calls promptly, and do what must be done to keep the process flowing smoothly, you have a right to expect the same of your loan officer. If you behave in an opposite manner, do not be surprised if he responds in kind. <u>Act the way you expect to be treated and expect no less than to be treated the way you act.</u>

Also, before he is able to do anything for you, a loan officer must be confident of at least two things. First, that he is able to get you *some* kind of loan (which means you'll need to answer some qualifying questions at the outset); and second, that you are being honest about your credit, income, job history, cash available, etc. All programs have qualifying requirements, and the quotes you receive while shopping around will be based upon the information you provide to the lender. As they say in the computer industry: "garbage in, garbage out." If you are less than forthcoming about certain issues, you may receive a quote based on a program for which you cannot qualify, or that is not applicable to the type of transaction you wish to do. Then you're simply wasting everyone's time, including your own, and setting yourself up for disappointment.

# Step 2: Recognize What You're Paying For.

*close*

There are only two categories here: service and product. Costs for the former are referred to in mortgage industry jargon as "non-recurring," and those for the latter as "recurring." In a mortgage transaction the "product" is the money you're borrowing, and the interest rate is its basic cost. It is the most straightforward aspect of the two categories. The lender provides you with funds for a specific purpose, under specific terms, and as long as you have an outstanding balance, you agree to pay a certain percentage of each dollar owed in interest. If you borrow one dollar at an annual rate of 7.5%, you will owe 7.5 cents per year for every year you hold onto that dollar. To carry it further, if you borrow $100,000 at the same rate, you will owe $7,500—or 7.5% of the outstanding balance—for every year you keep the loan. Interest is a perfectly logical and reasonable way to pay for the use of money; it is a fixed percentage of every dollar owed. It's almost the same principle employed when you buy meat. If the price is one dollar per pound, then you pay one dollar for one pound, and twenty dollars for twenty pounds—the cost is directly related to the *amount* of product you receive. (The difference, of course, is that you don't have to bring the meat back to the butcher when you're finished with it.) Thus, with a mortgage you're not really "buying" the money, you're just "renting" it. Since you will owe interest for as long as you "rent" the mortgage funds, interest is an ongoing, or "recurring" cost. The money is the *only* tangible item you are getting in a mortgage transaction, everything else comes under the category of *service*.

So, what sort of service are you receiving? Well, the investors who buy mortgage loans do not have branches or storefronts, they have no retail salespeople, they do not deal directly with the public. In order to sell a mortgage to a secondary mortgage market investor, you must be able to sell in bulk. Fannie Mae, Freddie Mac, and all the others, purchase loans in large quantities; and in order to deal with them you must be prepared to meet strict financial qualifications, warrant the loans you sell as far as performance and quality, and promise to deliver certain minimum amounts. Obviously, individual borrowers are unable to do this. Therefore, your lender is providing a valuable service by acting as the middleman between you and the ultimate investor; and the primary source of payment for that service is the origination fee, and other miscellaneous fees that I will explain below.

There are numerous service providers needed to bring the transaction to a successful close, one of the most important of which is your loan officer—whose paycheck is part or all of the origination fee. The remaining fees will, for the most part, be charged by various third parties for things such as an appraisal, escrow service, title insurance, a credit report, inspection of the property, etc. I will show you how to negotiate all of them in the next section. Here, I want to point out that, just as you will be comparing prevailing rates to determine if what you're getting is fair, you should be comparing service for the same reason. It is crucial that you understand exactly how you are being charged, and what you will get in return.

The cost of money, as with the cost of meat, is a direct, one-to-one relationship: the more meat you buy, the more money you pay. Likewise, the more money you borrow, the more interest you pay. The price per pound (or dollar) does not change, only the total cost, based upon how much product you purchase. A service, on the other hand, is a bit more difficult to quantify. The best way to illustrate this is with an example. Let's go back to our $100,000 mortgage. If a one percent origination fee is charged, the borrower will pay $1,000 in exchange for the bank arranging an investor, and the loan officer taking the application and processing the paperwork. On a $200,000 loan, the *same* one percent *doubles* the commission to $2,000; yet, the amount of paperwork, time, and effort involved on behalf of the bank and the loan officer will not have changed at all. It's basically a matter of erasing the "1" and filling in a "2" then collecting an extra grand for the trouble! The point I'm trying to make is that you should not judge the fairness of service fees by the *amount* of the loan. Instead, you should negotiate based upon the level of service required and expected, which brings us to the next step in the process.

# Step 3: Know Thyself!

By now I hope you've come to understand that the origination fee is actually the lender's (and loan officer's) *commission*, that this fee is charged for the *service* of providing the loan (not for the actual money itself), and that it is ordinarily calculated—and quoted—using a *percentage* of the loan amount. In order to ensure you are paying a reasonable amount for this service, you must see past the "package deal" that the industry offers up as the normal and customary method of calculating this fee. You must discard the notion that the size of the *commission* should be directly related to the *amount* you wish to borrow. Instead, you should focus on what will be required in terms of knowledge, experience, skill, and effort, on the part of your loan officer, to get the deal done. However, not all borrowers are created equal, and how you rate on the qualification scale will play a leading role in determining what you will pay for service.

Here is where you must be brutally honest with yourself; if you are not, you will lose one of the most valuable aspects of your negotiating power. If you underestimate your quality as a borrower, you are much more likely to over pay. However, contrary to what it may seem, overestimating your quality as a borrower has the same, not an opposite effect. If you think you are more qualified than you actually are, and you act accordingly, you will only waste a great deal of time pounding your head against walls you should not even be facing. You will also be likely prey for unscrupulous salespeople, who will have no compunction about promising you whatever you want to hear, until you've been maneuvered into a position from which you are unlikely, or unable to extricate yourself; at which point you will be subject to their control. I will illustrate how that is possible as we go on. First, I'm going to give some guidelines by which to evaluate yourself. This is the same way any good loan officer will evaluate you before giving you a quote.

Lenders use the "Three C's" to evaluate you as a borrower: Character,  Capacity, and Collateral. "Character" covers every aspect of your profile that relates to your *willingness* to pay back your debts, the most significant indicator of which being your credit history. "Capacity" encompasses anything that evidences your *ability* to repay; cash is king in this category—the more you have and the more you're earning, the better you look. "Collateral" is the lender's failsafe; it is the means by which he will collect what he is owed in the event that the first two C's fall short of expectations. In the case of a mortgage, the collateral is always the Real Estate. Let's cover them one at a time.

How is your credit? If you can honestly answer "true" to all of the following questions, then you are "A" quality as far as credit is concerned. Your willingness to repay your debts has been amply documented, and there are no "clouds" or "issues" on your record that may require you to jump through an extra hoop or two. However, if you miss even one, please obtain a copy of your credit profile from all three credit repositories, and study it carefully *before* proceeding with any mortgage transaction; because there is a great deal more to a credit profile than a history of punctual payments. In fact, you may possess a perfect payment record on every penny you've ever borrowed and still represent a credit risk to a lender—so, don't skip the test either! (For more on obtaining a credit report, see *Part IV*.)

1.     Within the past thirty days, I have obtained a copy of my credit profile from Experian, Trans Union, and Equifax, and all three are completely free of any type of derogatory item. True/False

2.     There has never been a late payment recorded on any debt I've ever had. (This includes recorded late payments that

were not your fault, and errors that were later removed). True/False

3. I have had little or no consumer debt (credit cards, auto loans, student loans, personal loans, etc.) for the past two years or more. True/False

4. I have never acted as a co-signer on a loan for another person (friend, family or otherwise). True/False

5. My name is not the same as, or very similar to any other family member or relative ("junior," "senior," "II," "III," same first and last with different middle initial, etc.) True/False

6. No other person (family member or otherwise) ever picks up my mail for me. True/False

7. I have never received a pre-approved credit card solicitation in the mail and thrown it into the trash without shredding it. True/False

8. I have never lost my wallet or purse, a credit or ID card, drivers license, or any other item that contains personal information about me, or thrown old bank statements, deposit slips, credit card statements, etc., into the trash without shredding them. True/False

9. I have always paid all my medical and dental bills in cash at the time the service was rendered, and never allowed the physician, dentist, hospital, etc., to bill my insurance company. True/False

10. I have never returned an item purchased on a credit card or disputed a charge shown on a monthly statement. True/False

11. I have no college-age or adult children that are still dependent, or semi-dependent upon me. True/False

12. I have never allowed a waiter, cashier, or other person to take my credit card out of my sight for even a moment. True/False

13.     I have no social security number, pay no taxes, have no drivers license, live in a box on the side of the road, and pay cash for everything. True/False

Didn't pass? Why does that not surprise me? I hope that little exercise has made my point for me: regardless of how perfect you *think* your credit history is, do not fail to verify that fact before proceeding to shop for a mortgage loan. I will illustrate with a personal anecdote. Some years ago, I worked for a well-known, regional lender (a portfolio lender, in fact) as a loan officer, and most of my clients were customers of the bank. I received a call one day from a woman inquiring about a refinance. After asking her a few qualifying questions, I determined that she and her husband (who were long-time customers of my employer) were excellent prospects, and we set an appointment to meet. After I had helped them complete the application, and collected income documentation, etc., I began the application process with the normal first step: I ran a credit report. Over the years, I have had countless clients tell me that their credit was perfect, only to retract that statement after a report turned up a couple of "dings" that they had "forgotten" about. In most cases, either they were telling the truth about their memory loss, or they had withheld the details hoping (or believing) they were too minor to matter. It happens so often, in fact, that new loan officers quickly learn to always take the borrower's own description of his credit history with a grain of salt, until it is verified by a credit report. In the case of these clients, however, even *I* was shocked at the extent of apparent denial on the part of the borrowers—their credit was absolutely horrible! They had dozens of revolving credit accounts, all charged up to the limit, and not a single one without a string of late payments going back at least two years. They also had a mortgage on a second home that had apparently *never* been paid on time since its inception. I was frankly amazed that anyone could look me straight in the face and casually say "my credit is perfect" knowing I would run a report and see what I saw! As it turned out, my clients really *were* oblivious to the state of their financial affairs. They had been the victims of a fraud that was, even then, still ongoing; and the worst part was that it was their own daughter and son-in-law who had done this to them. They actually lived next door, in a house the parents had built and given to them as a wedding gift! The mortgage on that house was in the parents' names, but the children were supposed to be making the payments. The daughter was in the habit of picking up the parents' mail, and had intercepted, and applied for, dozens of pre-approved credit card offers directed to them. She obtained her father's social security number, forged his signature, and listed herself as an additional borrower. She was able to keep it all secret from them by putting her phone number and address on the applications, and always making sure to get to the mailbox before anyone else.

Fortunately, the story had a happy ending: after six months, and six denials, I was able to get them their loan. But not without a heroic effort on my part to help them prove to their creditors that the derogatory accounts were fraudulently obtained, and to convince my employer that they were indeed a good risk. This is, of course, an extreme case; but it serves to illustrate the importance of monitoring your credit profile, and how critical it is to choose a loan officer who will be an advocate rather than an adversary.

Now, don't worry that you won't be able to get a loan if you have had (or now have) issues with your credit. There are loans for all types of borrowers, even those who have just emerged from bankruptcy or foreclosure. You just have to realize that, as a general rule, the worse your credit problems, the more it is going to cost you in terms of time and effort, rate, fees, and available cash (or equity) to make the deal. If you have any kind of credit problems, regardless of severity, take extra care to be accurate here. The thing to remember about the "Character" category is that *any* issue that tells the lender something about your willingness to pay will be evaluated. So be honest with yourself, and don't pull any punches; and you'll be in a much better position to choose the proper person to work with and to negotiate a fair commission.

Now let's talk about "Capacity." Cash, in all its forms, is "Capacity" to a lender. The amount you have, and the amount you earn both play a big part in your ability to qualify for a loan. The less you have of either, the fewer choices you'll have, and the more work your loan officer will have to do. Therefore, if you have no down payment, and make a modest income, understand that it is reasonable for your loan officer to expect a higher commission (regardless of loan size), due to the extra experience, knowledge, and effort required of him—especially if you *also* have credit problems. Conversely, those of you in Mr. A's league have plenty of spare cash and lots of disposable income; you should expect to pay less because your loan will require much less time, effort, skill, experience and knowledge to close. That's assuming, of course, that you're not attempting to do a super-jumbo refinance on a mixed-use commercial building that combines a shopping mall and condominiums in one structure, and hoping to get cash out! But even then, you'll have an easier time than someone on the opposite end of the spectrum attempting to qualify for the same loan. Once again, don't fall into the trap of negotiating the commission based upon the loan amount. Evaluate your capacity as objectively as possible, and expect to pay a commission that is reasonably commensurate with the work involved in your case. (For some guidelines on what lenders expect in this area, see *Part IV*).

The last "C" is "Collateral." The Real Estate is, by definition, always the collateral in a mortgage transaction. However, despite its importance, of the three C's, the collateral tends to be the *least* understood; and most often forgotten, or marginalized by the borrower. You can have a platinum credit history, piles of extra cash, and a ponderous income, and still be unable to get a loan, if the property you wish to purchase doesn't qualify.

Yes, yes… I hear you're incredulous cries: "What! You expect me to believe that a property has to qualify, as if it were a human being?"

Of course!

This is because, although your lender is always counting primarily on *you* to pay back the loan, should you lose your job, or your business, or anything else that would render you unable to pay, the *house* will have to be sold to satisfy the debt. Therefore, the collateral is of great importance.

As a general rule, the better the physical condition of the house, and the less owed against the actual value, the easier it will be to get a loan. If you have little or no down payment or equity, you will qualify for fewer programs, and more will be required of your loan officer. Even Mr. A should expect to pay a higher commission if he wishes to finance the purchase of a broken down Beverly Hills mansion, or any property in need of major repairs, e.g., one that has earthquake damage. (For some guidelines on what lenders look for in collateral, see *Part IV*).

Once you've determined how you measure up as a borrower, you are ready to begin the shopping and negotiation process; but don't forget the rule for deciding on a fair price for services rendered: Service can be good, fast, or cheap; and not even the platinum Mr. A can do better than two out of those three. Regardless of your financial qualifications, *if you need the loan fast*, and you want good service, *it won't be cheap*; if you want it cheap and fast, the service will suffer; if you demand exceptional service, at a great price, be prepared to get in line and patiently wait your turn; because that is far and away the most popular combination—and the *hardest* to find. It's now time to revisit some familiar terms, and view them from another perspective.

# Part III

*Negotiating The Deal And*
*Making It Stick*

# *The GFE*

The first rule of negotiation is: get it in writing! It is also test number one for finding that honest, ethical, hard-working individual, who will ensure you get a great deal on a program that is perfect for you. Throughout this chapter I will be hammering this concept home, because it really is the *only* rule; every other rule finds its roots here. A verbal quote is not even a promise: it is simply bait designed to coax you into taking the next step, the one that brings you closer to that all important commitment. Ultimately, you will have to commit to *some* lender, and he to you. However, that commitment should take place *at the time you apply*, not later; and it should be *mutual*. If you allow your lender to delay his commitment to you until the balance of power has swung well onto his side, you are leaving your wallet open for plundering.

One of the first written documents you will be asking for is a "Good Faith Estimate"; and as the name implies, it is your first means of determining the lender's good faith (or should be, anyway!). In mortgage industry jargon, it is referred to as a "GFE". There is a standard form, called the HUD-1 (and also an abbreviated version called the HUD-1A, which is designed for refinances), on which mortgage lenders are required by law to list all the costs associated with the transaction at its close. A properly completed HUD-1 makes it easy for you to do meaningful comparisons between lenders, because HUD has categorized all the fees related to any Real Estate transaction and assigned each particular category a set of line numbers, which appear on the form. Items payable in connection with a mortgage, for example, are assigned to the 800's; and there are certain line numbers within the

800's that are reserved for specific fees (e.g., line 801 is always the origination fee); but lenders are not limited as to the amount or type of fees they may charge, nor what they may call them. Therefore, if your lender decides to charge you a "Whatchamijiget Fee," he may do so without limitation, as long as you agree to it, and it appears on the appropriate line in the 800 section of the HUD form. This requirement enables you to directly compare quotes from different lenders; because if the GFE from one shows a $250 "Funding Fee" on line 808, and the one from Lender B shows a $150 "Research Fee" on the same line, you can rest assured that it is the same fee with different names, and that Lender B is cheaper. The problem is that RESPA does *not* require lenders to use the standard form if a borrower has not yet *applied* for a loan. Therefore, if you ask for a GFE while you're still shopping around, it may come in almost any format. Lenders sometimes have their own standardized, internal forms; but the forms are not standard between companies; and loan officers often make up their own, which makes it difficult to do direct comparisons between quotes from different lenders. So, if you receive a quote on the lender's, or loan officer's own form (instead of the HUD-1 or HUD 1A), make sure it has the RESPA line numbers, or you may find yourself attempting to compare apples to oranges. (See The Appendix for a sample HUD-1 and HUD-1A.)

Another step you must take in order to ensure that the GFE's you get will be useful, is to always use the same variables when asking for a quote. For example: if you're doing a purchase, give the same purchase price and down payment, and always ask for the exact same loan terms. When you are asked qualifying questions, always state the same income, cash available, etc. If you change any of the variables between quotes, you will be left trying to compare buses to baby buggies (i.e., both are vehicles, but that is about all they have in common with each other). And remember, it is not yet crucial that you get a quote which exactly matches the program and terms that you will ultimately take. Your main goal at this point is to compare identical programs offered by different lenders in order to discover who has the relatively lower prices, and to find the right *person* to work for you.

Here, I wish to add a side-note about jargon: I throw it around throughout this book, and don't be afraid to pick it up and use it yourself. I can assure you that your treatment will be based, in part, upon the loan officer's perception of your relative level of knowledge and experience. Compare the way the following two borrowers approach a lender:

> Borrower 1.) Hello, this is Mr. Iggy Noramus. I was wondering if I could get some information about a home loan. I'm thinking about buying a house and this is the first time for me. I really have no idea where to start. Can you help me out?
>
> Borrower 2.) Hello, this is Dr. Moneybags. I'd like to get a quote on a $180,000 conventional, fixed-rate mortgage with a fully amortized, fifteen-year term. Give me the par rate with no more than a one-percent origination fee, and no pre-payment penalty. It will be a purchase transaction with twenty percent down. Please make sure the quote is on a HUD-1 and fax it to my office.

Who do you think is more likely to end up with higher costs? Well, the truth is that either one could be taken advantage of if he fails to shop around and neglects to get his quotes in writing. However, all else being equal, an unscrupulous salesperson would consider Borrower One easy prey and be much more careful with Borrower Two.

Getting back to the GFE... The Real Estate Settlement Procedures Act (RESPA) requires mortgage companies to provide borrowers with a Truth-In-Lending disclosure, which includes a GFE, within three days of the date of application. However, no such requirement exists while you're still shopping around; and good loan officers customarily use this fact as their first opportunity to get you to commit to them. You ask for a written cost estimate, and they respond by saying that the company requires borrowers to apply first. Instead of meekly complying, or simply moving on to another lender, I want you to turn things around. Use this as your first opportunity to test the honesty of the person with whom you may be dealing, and his willingness to commit to you. Now, I don't want you to think that just because a loan officer attempts to get you to commit at the outset, he is automatically preparing to take advantage of you. Any good salesman will have that goal foremost in his mind; and good salesmen are, quite often, the most experienced, i.e., the most *capable* of doing a good job for you. If you are asked to apply before a written quote will be given, I want you to respond that you'll be happy to provide any information the loan officer needs in order to prepare an accurate quote, but you'd like to shop around before making a commitment. His response will be telling: If he refuses, it's a no-brainer, just move on to the next lender. This is just basic common sense; since a written quote will *always* have conditions such as a time frame within which it is good; disclaimer language that identifies it as an estimate, rather than a commitment; and requirements for verification of income, credit, etc., that must be met before any commitment will be made. The conditions are what differentiates it from a binding contract. Therefore, written quotes can be verified for their veracity within their limits, and someone who will not put a quote in writing is literally saying that he can't, or *won't* stand by his word, i.e., he's probably not telling the truth.

There is one more thing you should be looking for in this step: the loan officer should ask you to answer some basic qualifying questions. This is extremely important, because an unqualified quote may not be one that is applicable to your situation. If the loan officer just asks you for the specific product and terms you want, and prepares the quote based on program information alone, he is either inexperienced or simply willing to tell you anything you wish to hear in order to get you to the next step—neither one of which is good for you. An experienced (and honest) loan officer knows that he cannot make an accurate quote without establishing, at least verbally, that you can actually *qualify* for the product/terms you are requesting. Here is where you must be willing and able to provide information about your income, employment, credit history, etc. If a loan officer asks you for basic  qualifying information up front, then provides you with a written GFE (at no cost, and without requiring you to apply), and it matches his verbal quote, he passes the initial character/competency test. If the written quote is in any way different from what was quoted to you verbally, you may give the loan officer the benefit of the doubt—*once* (administrative errors do occur!), but do not proceed until it is corrected.

In addition to presenting your first opportunity to qualify the loan officer, the GFE will be invaluable in making comparisons of costs. Unlike your own scribbled notes, or allegedly photographic memory, written estimates from various lenders can be laid side by side on your kitchen table and compared directly.

This brings me to another important aspect of the "balance of power" that I did not discuss earlier: knowledge. In order to negotiate any fee, you must know four things: (1) who is charging it, (2) how it is calculated, (3) what purpose it serves, and (4) what is the upper and lower range of "normal and customary" for that fee. The GFE will help you fortify your power base of knowledge in all these areas, and particularly that of number four. With this knowledge, you'll have a means of deciding if the "those fees are standard, sir" response is acceptable to you. Instead of going by a vague, gut feeling, that you're being ripped off, you'll be able to know with confidence that what you're being offered is reasonable. If it is not, you'll have written quotes from competing sources that can be used to shore up your request for a reduction. Since it is unlikely that you will find one lender who will have the lowest rate, the lowest fees, the perfect program, and the most outstanding service, these written estimates from other lenders will help you make your case with the one who comes closest to meeting all your needs. In the course of your comparison shopping, you will probably narrow the field to two or three finalists. One will be the best on points, the other on fees, another on service, etc. It will then be up to you to negotiate with them to come up with a winner willing to deliver the best possible package for your circumstances; and one of the best ways to accomplish this is to produce written evidence of a competitor's program. If the lender doesn't normally negotiate a particular fee; and you have proven yourself to be, not only qualified as a borrower, but ready to commit to the right deal, presenting a competitor's quote can be quite effective. After all, less of *something* is better than all of *nothing*. But please don't try this if you have not followed all the previous steps, including the most important: an honest self-evaluation. Because it won't work if the lender is not confident that he can actually do a deal for you, and that you are willing to commit to him if it is offered.

# *Negotiating The Origination Fee*

For most loan officers, the origination fee (i.e., commission) is their only source of income. They are, therefore, highly motivated to close every loan they can. If a loan doesn't close, they earn nothing, despite any time and effort they've already spent working on it. In this sense, the loan officer is your advocate; because, like you, he has a stake in the success of the transaction. It is this vested interest that you must simultaneously cultivate and constrain. If your self-evaluation has led you to conclude that your case will require someone with a good deal of expertise and a strong work ethic, or you simply desire to have an experienced hand to hold because it's your first time out, you will definitely want a traditional loan officer working for you. If, on the other hand, you are an experienced and savvy Mr. A, you may not necessarily need to pay the additional cost of personal service. However, it is important to note that there are two aspects to the concept of service: "smiles" and "smarts." "Smiles" is my term for the courtesy, respect, deference, fair dealing, etc., you should demand, and *expect*, no matter what amount you're paying for the commission. No special experience, training, or skill is required for this aspect of service (albeit some people are more talented in this regard than others), and it should not cost you one penny more to be treated with due care and attention. You should, however, expect to pay more if you desire—or require— above average knowledge, skill, experience, and competence (i.e., "smarts") from your loan officer. Here I wish to point out the difference between a traditional mortgage lender, and what I would term a "discounter." The basic distinction is service—the "smarts" kind. In a nutshell, you get what you pay for. A "wholesale-to-the-public" outlet may be a great place to buy meat, but mortgages are an animal a bit more complicated in nature. The countless internet lenders that have sprung up recently (and vanished just as quickly) exemplify mortgage discounters: They keep their overhead low by replacing brick and mortar branches, and human beings, with automation and electronics wherever possible. They advertise bargain basement rates and costs, and work on the narrowest possible margins, hoping to capitalize on the principle of economy of scale through massive volume. This is a valid, useful, and timely concept—for *some* borrowers. If you are the generic Mr. A, as are the property, loan amount, and all other aspects of the transaction; and you are prepared to carry out many of the duties of a loan officer yourself; then you will save some money here. However, proceed with caution if you are a first-time buyer, self-employed, have past or current credit problems, are financing a unique or non-conforming property, etc. In other words, be ready to do-it-yourself as a trade-off for low cost. This is especially true on a purchase transaction, because at some point, you will be contractually obligated to complete the sale, or experience a financial loss. If "Cyber-Loans, Inc." fails to get an expected round of financing needed to keep it afloat for another quarter in a sagging market, and decides to close its electronic doors in the middle of your deal, you will have some scrambling to do—especially if you have an approved loan and your good-faith deposit is at risk of being forfeited to the seller. Think it won't happen to you? When my last employer (a high-profile "dot com" company) gave me and the entire mortgage division pink slips on two days notice, I had to walk away from a twelve million dollar pipeline of loans in progress (most of which were purchase transactions), and there was no mortgage division left to process them. They sat a good long time in limbo until the company was able to negotiate their sale to another, healthier mortgage company. Many hopeful homebuyers had to cancel their escrows and start over again from scratch. But maybe that was just me....

Once you know how you rate as a borrower, you are in a position to negotiate a reasonable commission. In order to do this, you must let the loan officer know, at the outset, that you wish to pre-negotiate it. Remember that his self-interest can help you or hurt you here; if you go too high, you'll be hurting yourself; but if you go to low, you're less likely to get the service you expect. The main thing to remember is that the commission should be based upon the *service* level required, which is not necessarily related to the loan amount. Don't be afraid to negotiate a flat fee; and, of course, get-it-in-writing! The way you sell this to the loan officer is by pointing out that he does not have to worry about anything changing during escrow. For a commissioned loan officer, change is a double-edged sword; if rates drop, he always looks like a hero, and can often squeeze in a little extra profit without your knowledge; but when rates go up, he often has to convince his borrowers that he is not trying to take advantage of them, and may end up cutting his commissions in order to pacify them. If you show him that you are willing to pay a fair price for services rendered, regardless of the vagaries of the market, you offer him peace of mind. Thus, he won't have to worry about how much he'll make or lose, if such-and-such changes; and he will be free to concentrate on getting the job done.

Lastly, it is especially important to always pre-negotiate the commission if you choose a "zero points" or "zero cost" program; because, although it will be rendered invisible, you will still be paying it; and unless you've gotten your loan officer to commit to a certain amount in advance, you will have given up the right to know how much you'll be paying him. (For a sample commission agreement, see *The Appendix*).

# Negotiating Third Party and Lender Fees

Aside from the origination fee, there can be literally dozens of other non-recurring service fees involved in any mortgage transaction. They come in two basic categories: those that get paid to the lender, and those that go to various third parties (see *Part I* for examples). These fees, like all others, are negotiable; but how do you go about negotiating them? Let's talk first about third party fees. If you feel like a small (and confused) fish in a gigantic ocean here, your feelings are justifiable. Often, the borrower doesn't even know who they all are, much less have any say in choosing third party service providers. In the vast majority of mortgage transactions it is the loan officer and Realtor who pick the title and escrow companies, order the credit report and appraisal, recommend a home inspector or termite company, etc.; and the borrower who simply accepts what is presented to him. It is rare for a borrower to take an active role in choosing a particular company for a third party service, and even more rare for that same borrower to use a particular third party service provider more than once. The end result is that the third party service providers don't really have much interest in the individual borrowers in any given transaction. Instead, it makes much more sense for them to romance the lenders and Realtors; because *they* are the ones deciding who will be the beneficiaries of most of their business—and they do a whole lot more of it than any one borrower can ever hope to generate!

Since, as a borrower, you don't have any inherent power position with third party service providers, your primary power card for negotiating them will be knowledge of what the competition is offering. In *Part I*, I showed you how to gain that knowledge and simultaneously test the character of loan officers by asking for written quotes; now let's talk about how to use what you have gained. Loan officers and Realtors are constantly being solicited by representatives of title and escrow companies, appraisers, etc., who seek their business (which is ironic because it is not really *their* business—it is *yours*), and the more business a loan officer or Realtor generates, the more desirable he is to these third parities; consequently, the more influence he has over them. This influence can be used in one of two ways: two enrich the loan officer (or Realtor), or to benefit you. Obviously then, one of the first things you should look for is a loan officer who uses his influence to get discounts from third party service providers, and passes the savings on to his customers. However, be wary of the man wearing all the hats! I'm sure you've at least heard of the sort. He's the one who, as a Realtor, wears the hat of a "buyer's agent" in order to help you find a house, then proceeds to direct you to one of his own listings (at which point he dons the hat of the "seller's agent"); and of course, the purchase agreement will require that his in-house escrow company be used; he'll also act as your loan officer through his in-house lender; he's a licensed appraiser, so he'll take care of the property evaluation; and as a notary, he'll perform the signing procedure at the time of closing. Now, having all these services under one "hat" may be a very convenient and beneficial arrangement; but the question is: who does it benefit—you, or him? There is only one way to find out: you must compare the "package deal" to its competition. If it actually is a better deal, then dive right in! But please don't accept it at face value simply on the assumption that "package deals" as such are inherently less costly.

Now, what about the lender fees? As discussed in the previous paragraph, third party service providers put their primary focus on lenders and Realtors. Thus, to gain any meaningful influence over them, one must do so indirectly, through the lender and Realtor. The lender fees, however, are a different story. Here the borrower himself has quite a bit more influence, because the lender's primary focus is on him; but in order to exercise that influence, he must know what the lender's competitors are offering. This is yet another reason why a written quote from a lender is far superior to a borrower's own scribbled notes. Unlike the latter, a lender's written quote carries the weight of reality with a competitor. In other words, you are much more likely to get a lender to come down on a given fee, or fees, if you can prove that someone else is already willing to do so. Also, a good loan officer will be able to spot the "catch-22's" in a competitor's written quote, and therefore provide valuable information you will need in order to decide which is best.

So, what's the bottom line? There are two lessons to be learned here: knowledge is *potential* power, and commitment is *actual* power. Knowledge is relatively easy to gain with even a moderately diligent effort, but in order to become useful, it must be applied. In the case of mortgage loans, the application of power is accomplished through commitment; and this principle applies to all phases of a mortgage transaction. In the beginning, when you are shopping around for a lender, you gain information by providing it; but you get what you give (i.e., it is tentative, conditioned upon verification and a potential future commitment). When you decide to commit to a lender by applying with him, you are now offering him something much more valuable than a *potential* commission. Your commitment converts you to an *actual* client; and as such, you are entitled to a commensurate commitment from your lender, and now wield a commensurate influence over him—and therefore his fees. Consequently, although it is crucial to gain knowledge up front, before you commit to a lender, you will not be able to exercise its full power until you are ready to apply.

# Determining and Verifying The Cost Of A Discount

Earlier I demonstrated how you could find yourself on the wrong side of the "Balance Of Power" and end up paying a higher commission that is hidden within the cost of discount points. If you are learning anything at all, by now you should understand that the best defense is a good offense. If you do your comparison-shopping up front, get a commitment in writing from your lender at the time of application, and verify everything before proceeding, you will never find yourself in that position. However, should you end up in a situation similar to that of Don and Donna Jumbo, there is hope. In fact, as long as you haven't signed your loan documents, it's not too late to correct things. Just remember that you can apply the principles I will now describe at any time prior to that; but the best practice is do so before committing yourself to a lender.

The best method by which to determine and verify the cost of a discount is to ask the loan officer to provide you with a copy of the wholesale rate sheet from which he is quoting you. The best time to get this is at the time the quote is given, while you're still comparison-shopping. Unfortunately, you're not likely to get it then, because the loan officer will probably be fired if he provides it for you. That information is not normally available for scrutiny by the general public, and there are two major reasons for this: The first—and most obvious—is the lender's profit-motivated desire to keep his costs confidential from his clients. This is perfectly reasonable and to be expected; there is nothing illegal, unethical, or immoral about running a profitable business (although it certainly may be fattening if one is good at it!). The second is the lender's survival-motivated desire to keep his costs confidential from his competitors. After all, there is no guarantee that you will not disclose his rate sheet to his competition after you get it. In fact, that is probably precisely what you will do. There is nothing unreasonable about this motivation either. However, for your own protection, you need to have some means of evaluating a quote. Therefore, I'm going to give you a formula to use for that purpose.

This formula is a rule-of-thumb that I have developed over more than a decade of following mortgage rates. It is not an industry standard, a strict rule, company policy, or even a general guideline; it is simply a comparison tool that will get you close enough to make a judgment. It is the same formula I myself would use to estimate the cost of a discount when I know the prevailing rates, but have no rate sheet handy to check. You will be able to verify the actual cost once you commit to a lender; prior to that, you'll have to apply the formula. Here's how it works.

First, you must determine how much your interest rate is going to be discounted. For example, if the prevailing rate is 7.5% and you need 7.0%, then you will need a rate discount of one-half percent (7.5% minus 7.0% = 0.5%). Second, you multiply the amount of the discount times three (0.5% x 3 = 1.5%). You have now arrived at an average cost, but you're not finished; because, since this is a rule-of-thumb, you must apply a margin of error. Experience has shown me that the average cost of a discount can vary as much as 0.25% (¼ percent) up or down on any given day, due to fluctuating market conditions. Therefore, you must take the average (1.5% in this case), and add a quarter, then subtract a quarter, to arrive at a range (1.5% + 0.25% = 1.75%, and 1.5%—0.25% = 1.25%). If the quote you receive falls within the range, then it is not likely that the loan officer is trying to hide any additional commission in the discount. Let's review the steps:

1. Determine the amount of the discount. (Prevailing rate minus desired rate).
2. Multiply the amount of the discount times three to arrive at the average cost.
3. Add 0.25% (¼ percent) to the average cost to arrive at the high end of the range.
4. Subtract 0.25% (¼ percent) from the average cost to arrive at the low end of the range.
5. Compare the result with the discount cost given.

Remember that the quote you receive will probably combine the lender's commission and the discount cost into one number. Therefore, in order to correctly figure the discount cost, you must subtract the lender's commission (origination fee) from the points quoted. Don't be afraid (and do not fail) to ask what portion of the points is going toward the lender's commission! You have a right to know how much you will be paying for his services, and you must have that information in order to make a meaningful comparison. This is another opportunity for you to test the forthrightness of the person with whom you may be dealing. If he is hesitant to reveal to you how much he is asking to be paid, you have good reason to wonder about what else he may not wish to tell you. Remember, you're still shopping now. You should not be as concerned yet about the ultimate rate and fees as you are about the *person* who will be responsible for delivering them to you. This formula will be a useful tool in helping you to distinguish those who make promises from those who make good on them.

Once you've decided upon a lender and committed yourself to him, you have a legal and ethical right to receive written verification of the deal you have struck. At this point, since you are definitely going to do business with him, and proven it by making an application and providing income, expense, and asset documentation, etc., you may ask for a copy of the rate sheet from which your loan officer has quoted you—and he should provide it. If he is unwilling, you have every right to assume that he has been leading you down the garden path and has no intention of delivering what he promised. If that is the case, it is not too late to back out, and you should do so with haste. If he complies, and everything stands up to scrutiny, then he has passed a crucial test of character, and you have secured your deal.

I'd like to add a final note on this subject before we move on. As we learned earlier, the Real Estate Settlement Procedures Act (RESPA) requires lenders to provide borrowers with a full disclosure of all costs on a standardized form within three days of application. The standardized form (HUD-1) will be yet another means by which you can verify the discount cost. It is here that the lender is required by law to disclose the exact amount of his commission and the discount charge on separate lines. The commission will appear on line 801, and the discount on line 802. The charges appearing on those lines should agree with what you've been promised; if they do not, get them corrected before proceeding.

# *Determining and Verifying The Amount Of An Overage*

Unlike the origination and discount fees, the law does not require lenders to disclose the amount of an overage. This is because it is paid to the lender only when, and if, the mortgage is actually sold (which cannot occur until after the loan has closed). It is, therefore (in the eyes of the law), a profit realized upon the sale of the negotiable instrument which you created when you signed your loan documents. Neither the original lender, nor the ultimate owner of the note can change the terms you agreed to (i.e., the interest rate, monthly payment, etc.), but they can transfer the right to benefit from those terms (i.e., the right to receive the interest payments). If your lender realizes a profit upon the sale of those rights, it is his to keep; if he experiences a loss, it is his to absorb. You have no direct interest in, or control of that aspect of the transaction. It is perfectly reasonable that the law operates in this manner; because there is no law which requires the lender to sell the note, nor any compelling an investor to purchase it. This does, however, create a caveat for you, the borrower. The caveat is that the note will indeed be sold; and the lender knows exactly how much he will get for it, and to whom it will be sold, before you even sign your loan documents. Which is why, in my opinion, it is dishonest for a loan officer to present a borrower with alternatives in a context that makes them appear balanced, when he knows one of them will cost his client more and generate a higher commission for him. (Refer back to *"Overage" The Invisible Fee* for my example of how this works).

Since there is no law requiring disclosure of an overage, it is critical that you get your lender to do so voluntarily. Furthermore, the market factors that drive overage prices vary considerably more than those that determine discount costs. Therefore, I have no formula that will provide you with any consistently reliable results as far as estimating the cost on your own. However, it can be done; and what's more, doing so will offer you yet another opportunity to test the character of your loan officer. There is really only one way to do it, and that is to ask for a copy of the wholesale rate sheet from which you are being quoted. However, for reasons stated earlier, you probably won't be able to get a lender to comply with that request while you are still shopping around.  Therefore, you must ask the lender to format your GFE in a specific manner: ask that the amount of the origination fee be listed as an actual charge on line 801 of the HUD-1, and the actual amount of the overage be shown as a credit from which an equal amount of your costs will be paid.

To further clarify, let's say you've decided to do a "zero points" loan. (As we learned earlier, this does not mean a zero commission loan; it just means that you agree to accept an above-market interest rate, and the lender agrees to take his commission out of the resulting overage.) I still want you to negotiate a set amount for the lender's commission, and that amount should be reflected on line 801 of the HUD-1.  Do not allow the lender to simply leave line 801 blank under the assumption that it will be paid from the proceeds of an undisclosed overage; because what this literally means is that they are not charging you an origination fee, which is not the case; and it does nothing at all to verify the actual amount the lender will collect. In other words, your lender won't have to tell you how much commission he's charging; but he'll be free to charge it nonetheless.

Once you've decided upon a lender, you will get-it-in-writing with a  Commission Agreement including verbiage specifically stating that any overages exceeding the amount of the agreed-upon commission will be credited toward your other closing costs. (A sample is included on the example commission agreement in *The Appendix*). At this point, you can also ask for the rate sheet from which you are being quoted. Once again, if any of the numbers disagree with the amount you've negotiated, you must get it corrected before you proceed. If that correction is not forthcoming, it is not too late to withdraw, and you should not hesitate to do so.

# *Requesting and Verifying A Rate Lock*

Now comes the <u>most important step of all</u>: <u>the lock</u>. It is at this point that you and your chosen lender finalize mutual commitments. If you leave this to the discretion of your lender, he will not lock your rate until your final loan documents have been requested; because final loan documents cannot be prepared until virtually everything required to assure the closing of the transaction has been completed (e.g., your credit has been checked, your job history and cash available have been verified, your income documented, the property value has been determined, its condition has passed muster, its title proven clear, etc., etc., etc.). At this point, all possible barriers to a successful conclusion have been removed, and the green light has been given to wrap it up. In a week or less, you'll be in your new home, or have your refinance completed. Your lender will wait until this point to lock, because he will now be able to deliver the closed loan to his investor within the short time frame required to avoid paying a lock fee; but for all the reasons  stated throughout this book, <u>you must not leave the timing of this crucial aspect of the loan process up to the lender</u>. To do so is to render worthless any time and effort you put into comparison-shopping and negotiating the deal up front. <u>If there is no lock</u>, t<u>here is no de</u>al.

You will have to commit at this point; but it is safe to do so if you've done your homework, found a good deal, and gotten it in writing. Yes, there is a chance that interest rates may drop, or stay the same during the time your loan is being processed. Therefore, there is a chance that the price you pay for the lock will be wasted, or even end up working against you; but how does that compare to the alternative? Before you can answer that question, you must understand a certain principle of any free market economy, which I call the "Wholesale/Retail Cost Information Gap." Here's how it works: Lenders borrow the money they lend, therefore, the cost of their funds is directly related to the ultimate retail price. If a bank borrows funds from the Federal Reserve at 5.75%, it must charge more than 5.75% to its mortgage clients in order to make a profit. If the Fed Chairman raises the prime rate, the bank's wholesale cost of funds goes up, and it must raise rates to its mortgage clients or go out of business; and the same process works in reverse when the Fed Chairman lowers rates. It is at the change point that the "Wholesale/Retail Cost Information Gap" comes into play. Since the profit motive is the driving force of a free economy, rising wholesale costs are quickly reflected in higher retail prices. No company will stay in business long if it does not react quickly to rising costs; but the same is not true when wholesale costs are dropping. In that circumstance, the longer a business can continue to collect the previously acceptable higher retail prices, the more profit it will make as the costs drop. Ultimately, it will have to fall into line in order to stay competitive; but there is always a window of opportunity created by the wholesaler's access to information that is not as readily available to consumers. Put yourself in the lender's place for a moment: You have a pipeline of customers with loans in progress, totaling twenty million dollars, all of whose loans will close in two days. For the purposes of simplicity, let's also assume that all your customers have already agreed to pay the prevailing rate of 7%, at which rate, you will collect only your commission and fees—no overage. Now, being in the mortgage business, you are acutely aware of fluctuations in the marketplace of money—especially those that will affect your bottom line. You receive information today that indicates your wholesale cost of funds will drop tomorrow, and indeed it does drop 0.25% (¼ percent) the very next day. You now have a choice; you can pass on the savings to your entire pipeline; or you can close them at the rate they are already expecting, and generate an overage of 0.625%, which will mean $125,000 in extra income on twenty million dollars. You have the information now; your customers probably won't become aware of it through the media for at least three or four days (if at all!). Which choice makes more sense for a free-market, profit-motivated (and smart!) business? Now, contrast that with the opposite circumstance: You, the lender, receive information indicating that wholesale rates will rise tomorrow; and indeed they do go up by 0.25%. If you allow your current pipeline of customers to close at the previous prevailing rate of 7%, you will now have to *pay* 0.625% on twenty million dollars to your investors to get them to purchase the loans at what is now a discounted rate. You can pay the $125,000 out of your own profit, collect the additional from your clients, or raise their rates; which would you choose? And how fast would you choose it? It is for this reason that rates always seem to rise faster than they fall.

The fact that market forces may work against you, and that lenders will always use their information advantage to hedge any changes in their favor, is reason enough to lock up front; but the Wholesale/Retail Cost Information Gap is not the only principle at work here. If you haven't gotten your negotiated deal in writing, and locked your rate, your loan officer is free to use any of the techniques I've shown you previously to increase his paycheck at your expense, including the Wholesale/Retail Cost Information Gap applied at the individual level. In other words, without a lock, not only will you be subject to the vagaries of market forces, you will also lack the protection it affords you against Caveat Emptor. In my opinion and experience, you will always stand to lose more money to either or both of those forces than you would have spent on a lock fee.

Besides, if you've negotiated a fair deal at the outset, and you were ready to live with it for the next fifteen to thirty years at that time, why would it suddenly become unacceptable three or four weeks later? My advice is to do your homework, make your deal upfront, get-it-in-writing, and lock it in. Then put your newspaper and magazine subscriptions on hold, turn off your television and radio, plug your ears when family, friends and co-workers bring up the subject of interest rates, accept what you've got, and sleep easy until your loan closes. Don't go into fits of anguished regret over drops of an eighth or a quarter, or even three eighths of a point in rates after you've locked; it's just not worth it! If your rate is not locked, you'll experience much worse anxiety, regret, and remorse, every time the rates tick *up* an eighth.

If you're still not convinced, bear in mind that the interest rate on a mortgage loan actually has very little bearing on how much you will ultimately pay in interest; because the terms under which you agree to pay back the debt are always the *minimum* requirements. There is no way of knowing exactly how long you will keep the loan; and there are many acceptable ways to repay a loan besides those spelled out in the contract. Let me illustrate with an example:

Mr. Lucky and Ms. Fortune have each decided to buy a home in the same new housing tract—in fact, they will be next-door neighbors when all is said and done. Their homes will be mirror images of each other in all aspects, including the price, which is $200,000. Both buyers will provide a $20,000 down payment, and get a thirty year fixed rate loan of $180,000 from the same lender, and will pay the same closing costs. The only difference is that Mr. Lucky's transaction closes on Tuesday, at an interest rate of 6.875%; and Ms. Fortune runs into a snag that delays her closing until Friday, at which point rates have jumped to 7.25%. My goodness, Mr. Lucky is way down in the 6's and Ms. Fortune is clear up in the 7's! Poor Ms. Fortune. It appears that she will be doomed to pay the 0.375% difference (a whopping $675 annually) for the next thirty years. Now, let's assume they both stay in their homes for the next thirty years, and neither one ever refinances. If both pay their loans according to the contract terms, Ms. Fortune will have spent

$20,250 more than Mr. Lucky. Okay, I'll grant you that twenty grand is nothing to laugh about, even spread out over three decades. Nonetheless, since it's my example, I'm going to introduce an alternative. I'm going to have Mr. Lucky make all 360 of his payments on the scheduled due date, in the scheduled amount of $1,182.47. After thirty years, he will have paid $245,691.50 in interest, plus the original balance of $180,000, for a grand total of $425,691.50. Ms. Fortune, on the other hand, has decided to do things a bit differently. She starts a "Christmas" account at her bank and begins to deposit $50 into it from each paycheck she receives. She is paid twice each month, so after a year the account value is $1,236 ($1,200 in deposits, plus $36 in interest at 3%). Each year, as a Christmas gift to herself, she withdraws the money from the account and makes an extra payment on her mortgage, instructing the lender to apply the entire amount to her principle balance. She keeps this up for twenty three years, at which point she will have made 305 payments of $1,227.92, and paid $195,677.47 in interest, plus the original balance for a total of $375,677.47. Since she no longer has a mortgage payment to make, Ms. Fortune decides to invest the same amount each month into a mutual fund account. Assuming she earns the historical stock market average of 9%, after seven years, she will have $142,962.95 in her portfolio; at which point Mr. Lucky has just made his last loan payment. He has made fifty-five more payments, paid $50,014.03 more in interest, and has no stock portfolio; but after all, he *did* have a lower rate.

The conclusion is obvious, but there is one more warning I must give you: Do not accept a anyone's verbal assurances that you have a lock. When your loan officer requests a rate lock, he will receive a *written* confirmation from the investor, which will contain, among other things: your name, the property address, the loan amount, interest rate, wholesale cost, date of the lock, and an expiration date. It is a *contract* in every legal sense. You must ask for a copy of that confirmation, and verify that everything is as it should be; because it is your last chance to test the character of your loan officer before the balance of power begins to shift. Should he fail to produce verification of your lock upon request, it is not too late to bail out; and you should do so with haste. If the requisite verification is forthcoming, and it withstands your scrutiny, your loan officer is well chosen, your deal is sealed; and you may proceed with confidence.

# *In A Nutshell*

Despite the mountains of verbiage you've just finished climbing, and the volumes of information contained therein, protecting yourself from unscrupulous salespeople is really quite simple; and it can be held in your mind with the acronym IPV:

1. Information – Shop and compare *before* you commit.
2. Person – In choosing a lender, put more weight on honesty and high ethics in the *person* than on the price and features of his *product*.
3. Verification – Get *everything* in writing (and make sure you actually *read* it!).

# Part IV

*FAQ's*

# *How Do I Obtain A Credit Report?*

There are three credit reporting companies: Experian (formerly TRW), Equifax, and Trans Union. Since some creditors do not report to all three, mortgage lenders require a special report that is a compilation of information from all three companies, which is called a "Three Repository Draw." There are a multitude of private companies that provide this service, none of which are affiliated with Experian, Equifax, or Trans Union; and when you pay a credit report fee to a mortgage company, it is one of these companies to which it will be paid. It is possible for you yourself to obtain a copy of your credit history directly from each of the three repositories; and I recommend that you do so *before* applying for a mortgage. If you have your own credit report, you will not have to worry about paying multiple lenders to run their own copies while you are shopping around; this will also mean that your credit history will be free of any inquiries from lenders to whom you talk, but with whom you do not ultimately apply. However, please bear in mind that your credit report will be dated, and the information contained therein will only be useful for about ninety days, after which you'll have to get an updated report. And when you decide on a lender, he will have to request a new Three Repository Draw, despite having seen the credit report you requested on your own. The following paragraphs explain how to go about requesting your own credit report from each of the major credit bureaus.

### Experian

A report may be obtained on the internet at *http://www.experian. com/consumer/index.html.* You will have to answer some personal questions for security purposes; and once granted access, you will be able to view your report on line, or print it out if you wish. There is no charge if you provide evidence that you have been denied credit within the past sixty days, otherwise the cost is $8.50 (a separate charge applies to each spouse for married couples). If you do not have access to the internet, you may request a report to be mailed to you by calling 800-311-4769 or by writing to the following address:

Experian
P.O. Box 9600
Allen, TX 75013.

### Equifax

A report may be obtained on the internet at *https://www.econsumer. equifax.com.* You will have to answer some personal questions for security purposes; and once granted access, you will be able to view your report on line or print it out if you wish. There is no charge if you provide evidence that you have been denied credit within the past sixty days, otherwise the cost is $8.50 (a separate charge applies to each spouse for married couples). If you do not have access to the internet, you may request a report to be mailed to you by calling 800-685-1111 or by writing to the following address:

Equifax
P.O. Box 740241
Atlanta, GA 30374.

**Trans Union**

A report may be obtained on the internet at *http://www.transunion. com/Consumer/*. You will have to answer some personal questions for security purposes before being granted access. You will then be able to order your report, but you will not be able to view it or print it out; it will be sent to you via U.S. Mail. There is no charge if you provide evidence that you have been denied credit within the past sixty days, otherwise the cost is $8.00 (a separate charge applies to each spouse for married couples). If you do not have access to the internet, you may request a report to be mailed to you by calling 800-888-4213 or by writing to the following address:

Trans Union
P.O. Box 390
Springfield, PA 19064

**The National Foundation for Credit Counseling**

The National Foundation for Credit Counseling is a non-profit organization that assists consumers in dealing with their credit problems. To find an office near you, call 800-388-CCCS (2227), or go to *www.nfcc.org*.

# How Much Cash and Income
# Do Lenders Expect?

This section is designed to give you general guidelines regarding the "Capacity" expected by mortgage lenders. Because of the number and variety of programs available—all of which differ on various specifics—I will not go into the finer details regarding debt ratios, reserve requirements, seasoning of funds, etc., of particular loan products. Instead, I will provide you with some principles by which you may *estimate* your Capacity as it relates to the type of loan you desire. If properly employed, they will aid you in objectively determining your relative attractiveness as far as capacity is concerned; which will prevent you from being fooled into thinking you're uglier (metaphorically speaking!) than you really are, and therefore agreeing to pay more than you should. You may also find that you are not quite as irresistible as you thought you were, and thereby save yourself much grief and frustration caused by the mistaken belief that everyone is out to rip you off.

There are three primary sub-categories of capacity: assets, income, and debt. The following paragraphs address each one in turn.

*Assets* come in two forms: liquid and non-liquid. The former comprise anything that can be turned into cash on short notice. Examples include checking, savings, certificates of deposit, and money-market accounts; stocks, bonds, and some retirement accounts. The key to being liquid is the ability to get your money out quickly. If you cannot convert the account to cash without declaring a hardship, quitting your job, retiring, losing a limb, or dying, it is not liquid as far as a mortgage lender is concerned. Non-liquid assets comprise anything that can be exchanged for cash at *some* point, but neither quickly nor easily. Examples include cars, boats, furniture, antiques, art, jewelry, stamps, coins, collectibles, business equipment, pedigreed pets, equity in Real Estate, the clothes on your back, your first born child, and anything else that could be sold or pledged. When it comes to assets, mortgage lenders favor liquid over non-liquid, except when it comes to equity in Real Estate. The old maxim about bankers refusing to lend you money unless you can prove you don't need it, is not *literally* true, but it serves to illustrate the principle: the more liquid assets, or equity you have, the more attractive you are to a lender, because you have a greater *capacity* to pay back the debt should you fall on hard times. There *are* loan programs for people who have virtually no liquid assets at all; however, the product choices are few; they often impose limitations on the amount of income you may be earning—or the areas in which you may buy—and they are *always* more expensive. As a general rule, the more liquid assets you have, the wider the range of products that will be available to you, the lower their cost, and the easier it will be for you to qualify. At minimum, you should have enough cash left over, after the transaction has closed, to make at least two loan payments (including principle, interest, taxes and insurance). Anything less will severely limit your options as to loan programs.

*Income* is any money that you have a documented history of earning, and will likely continue to receive into the foreseeable future. This means exactly what it says: if you are receiving income—regardless of the amount or source—but you have no way to *prove* you've been receiving it for at least two years, and/or no evidence indicating it will continue, it does not exist as far as a lender is concerned. This rules out income from a part-time or second job, or any source that has less than a two-year history that can be proven with documentation. You may run into the same problem if you've recently changed careers (as distinguished from changing employers but remaining in the same field), or started your own business, if you're paid in cash, by commission, or receive tax-free income. The cookie-cutter Mr. A works in a familiar career field; has been employed by the same company for the last two years, or more; earns a fixed salary with periodic pay raises; allows his employer to withhold at the maximum tax rate for his income level; and has no additional income from a second job, small business, etc. Lenders love the Mr. A's of the world because their income is easy to categorize, and verify; matches nicely with the questions next to the little boxes on the standard application forms; and plugs neatly into the programs used to process and qualify him. This is all well and good if you're a Mr. A; but what if you're self-employed, retired, or a recent graduate? How about those of you who are paid by commission, or in a career field that necessitates frequent changes of employers (such as an internet profession)? What if you're an investor and all your income is derived from stock gains, rental properties, or businesses that are run by people you hire? What if you have income from unverifiable sources, such as a boarder; or family members (such as parents) who live with you and contribute to the household expenses, but receive no taxable income? No problem! There are loan programs available for nearly every imaginable situation. There is even a category of products that do not require you to prove *any* income. Don't think that if you're not a classic Mr. A you will necessarily have a hard time getting a loan, or will have to pay exorbitant fees; it may actually be the contrary in some cases. The only way to know is to understand the principles involved so that you can clearly see where you stand in the lender's eyes, and know what to expect.

There are four basic questions to ask regarding your monthly income. Your answers will determine the choice of loan products available to you; and the relative level of experience, knowledge and effort that will be required from your loan officer. Let's analyze them one at a time:

1. *How much do you have left after all your monthly debt payments have been made?*

In general, the more discretionary income you have, the easier it will be for you to qualify for a loan; but this figure may have little to do with the actual amount you earn. I have done loans for professionals who make $20,000 to $30,000 per *month*; yet live such a high lifestyle they have little or nothing in savings, and mountains of debt that suck up every penny they take in. Conversely, I've had clients who barely earn that much in a year; yet have no debt, plenty of savings, and always seem to have extra cash. Lenders favor the latter for obvious reasons; but if you're like most people, you fall somewhere in between those two extremes. Just bear in mind that your place in the continuum will have a bearing on your ability to qualify, the number of programs available to you, and the amount you will ultimately pay for service.

2. *Can you provide hard evidence of the source of your income and its amount?*

The trade-off here is usually liquid assets or substantial equity. If you want a loan program that asks no questions regarding your income, be prepared to come up with at least twenty percent of the purchase price for a down payment; or if you're refinancing, you'll need that amount or more in equity. In both cases, you should have enough cash left over after close to cover six months of payments on the new mortgage, or more. This is, of course, the extreme; and there are programs that ask *fewer* questions, or require *less* documentation, and many variations on that theme comprising all levels from full-documentation to no-documentation of income. The rule is the more proof you have, the less money you need, and vice-versa.

3. *Do you have at least a two year, verifiable history of receiving the income?*

The longer you've been in one career field, with one employer, and the more traditional or familiar your profession, the better. If you've held four different jobs in the past twenty-four months, or just passed the bar exam and have a two month history in your first real job with a law firm; your going to need more cash, verifiable prospects for the future, or some combination of the two. For example: you began your first internship two months ago after having graduated from med-school; you've never held a real job in your life, but your future prospects are quite good indeed. As long as you're not being paid under-the-table, you'll probably be able to qualify as if you'd already been a working doctor for the past two years. Or maybe you're an investor: you don't have a *real* job in any traditional sense; you earn your living by finding "deals" (e.g., you buy old houses, rehabilitate them and sell them for a profit, play the stock market, or deal in privately owned classic cars, coins, collectibles, etc.). Whatever it is you do, it more than pays the bills; but it doesn't fit-the-box. Again, the more liquid assets you have, the fewer questions will be asked and vice-versa. Now, if you've held your present day job as a short-order cook at Denny's for two months, and your night job as a bartender at Hooter's for two weeks, but your "real" job is writing Hollywood screenplays—one of which is being looked at by the right people even as we speak—well, let's hope you're a talented author.

4. *Can you prove that the income is likely to continue into the foreseeable future?*

I'm sure I don't have to tell you that debt can be your ally or your adversary; and when it comes to the Capacity aspect of qualifying for a mortgage loan, your debts can only have a negative effect. The principle, simply stated, is: the more debt you have (as a percentage of your income), the harder it will be to qualify. The opposite is also true, all the way down to zero—no debt at all being the best. The only possible exception to that rule is someone who has no history of borrowing at all. However, even then, there are ways to use non-traditional means to establish a credit history. All else being equal, a borrower with an auto loan and a couple of credit cards may have an easier time qualifying than someone who has never borrowed a penny in his life; but this is simply due to the fact that the former has a proven history of responsibly handling debt, while the latter has none. This is not to say that you must be debt free before you can hope to get a loan. It means that any existing debt service payments take away income that would otherwise be available to make a mortgage payment. The key question a lender will seek to answer is: How much income do you have available to cover a mortgage payment after you've made the regular monthly payment to everyone else you owe?

The recent debut—and rapid adoption by most of the industry—of computer-generated decision-making (referred to as automated-underwriting), has drastically changed the way loans are approved. No longer are borrowers constrained to the limits of the traditional debt-ratio guidelines so heavily relied upon in the past (debt-ratio is jargon for the relationship between what you earn and what you owe). In the old days, to be classified as a Mr. A, a borrower's mortgage payment had to be no more than about a third of his gross income; and that, combined with all other monthly debt payments, had to fall within a range of thirty-three to thirty-eight percent (i.e., if you're gross monthly income is $100, you're total mortgage payment [PITI] should be less than $28; and that plus all other monthly debt payments should be less than $33). Automated underwriting uses statistical analysis to determine the manner in which a particular individual will likely repay his contract. Unlike a human underwriter—who must ultimately rely upon documentation, experience, and gut instinct—the computer program is able to compare one individual's credit, capacity, and collateral profile to thousands of similar individuals who now have mortgages—or have had one in the past. It then classifies the borrower in a manner that is highly indicative of future performance, regardless of social status, ethnic background, income level, job type, or neighborhood. In plain English, this means that the computer is able to be extremely objective; and it is most often correct.

Automated underwriting has taken a great deal of the guess-work out of approving loans, and has launched a new age of flexibility and opportunity for borrowers. Debt-ratios are becoming less important as more emphasis is put on the big picture. Nonetheless, it is not a panacea for the financially challenged; the old principles still apply, their boundaries have simply been expanded.

# What Do Lenders Expect From The Property?

With few exceptions, mortgage lenders have no interest in owning Real Estate; their primary focus is on finding borrowers who will pay on time, and who will keep the loan for as long as possible. Nonetheless, every mortgage transaction must, by definition, be secured by a property. Thus, the type, location, condition, and value of that property will play a key role in determining the rate, cost, terms, and qualifying guidelines of the loan. The lender's main concern will be the relative ease with which the property could be sold for enough to cover the loan in the event of default on the part of the borrower. There are four basic questions to consider:

1.  *Property Type*

Real Estate comes in a wide variety of forms; and although many of the principles discussed herein apply equally to commercial, industrial, recreational, and other types of property, the author assumes that most people reading this book are concerned with residential property—particularly that which is, or will be, the borrower's primary home. As a rule, the more similar the subject is to the majority of properties in its neighborhood, the easer it will be to finance. Style, square footage, number of stories, numbers of bedrooms and bathrooms, amenities, and lot size, all contribute to its relative conformity or uniqueness; but homogeneity is the main concern here. Despite your quality as a borrower, it will be much more difficult to find financing for the last remaining historical home in a neighborhood of apartment buildings, than it will be for the most popular model of a new housing tract that is nearly sold out.

2.   *Location.*

Location! Location! Location! It's the oldest axiom in the Real Estate business; and an axiom it is indeed. Structures come and go; land is eternal. Consequently, a desirable location will make nearly any property easier to finance, and vice-versa.

3.   *Property Condition*

Assuming a property is habitable, and not in blatant violation of building and safety codes, its condition should not make a significant difference in the type of loan required or the relative ease of qualifying. However, *major* problems such as earthquake or flood damage will have to be cured before standard financing will be allowed (in which case a construction loan is usually required). Nevertheless, there are some relatively minor problems that will completely hinder an otherwise uneventful transaction. Leaky roofs or plumbing; electrical problems; lead paint that is peeling, chipped, or cracked; exposed asbestos; and anything else that presents an actual, or potential, health or safety hazard, will bring your loan transaction to a grinding halt until it is repaired.

4.   *Property Value*

Value is one of the least understood aspects of Real Estate; and a major reason for this is the mixture of objectivity and subjectivity that is needed in order to evaluate a property. All the aforementioned factors relating to type, location, and condition come into play here; but regardless of the diligence, conscientiousness, objectivity, and attention to detail put forth in an effort to arrive at a number, it really all boils down to one question: How much is a ready, willing, and able *buyer* willing to *pay* for the property right now? Irrational emotions on the part of a buyer can wildly skew any objective appraisal of value. Consequently, mortgage lenders will always tend to err on the side of caution and assign a conservative value in ambiguous cases. As a borrower, you should bear in mind that conformity plays a large role in determining what it will take to get financing, and the most common property type in the immediate neighborhood will have the largest influence on the value of all others. Therefore, the relative value of the same two story, two-thousand square foot house, will be *lower* if it is located in a tract of mostly one story, one-thousand square foot houses, and *higher* if most of the neighboring homes are significantly larger. It reflects its most objective value in a neighborhood of similar homes.

# *The GFE*

## What May Change

*Non-Recurring Costs*: Any fee that is calculated using a percentage (i.e., "points"), or that is based upon the actual size of the loan, *will* change if there is a change in the loan *amount*, and *may* change if the loan is *not* locked. These include the origination fee, discount points, an overage/rebate, a lock fee, and some third-party fees, such as title insurance, and escrow.

*Recurring Costs:* The amount due at closing for pre-paid interest, hazard insurance, property taxes, and mortgage insurance will vary based upon the date of closing. An explanation of each follows:

## Pre-Paid Interest

Mortgage interest is customarily collected in arrears; which means that it will accrue for a given period of time (usually one month), and come due within a set number of days (usually fifteen) afterward. Therefore, a mortgage payment due on February 15$^{th}$, for example, will be credited toward interest that accrued from January 1$^{st}$ through January 31$^{st}$. Interest begins accruing from the day a loan closes, and billing cycles customarily end with the last day of each month. Thus, if your loan closes on January 25$^{th}$, your first billing cycle will end six days later on January 31$^{st}$; you would now owe six days worth of interest, and it would be due on February 15$^{th}$. However, to actually bill it this way would require a much speedier post-closing process than is usually possible; which is why your six days of accrued interest will be collected in advance, on the date your loan closes. The next billing cycle will then commence on February 1$^{st}$, interest will accrue through the last day of February; at which point the second billing cycle will end; and the first post-closing payment you make will not be due until March 15$^{th}$ (see calendars below). Your GFE will usually estimate fifteen days of pre-paid interest. Therefore, if your loan closes earlier in the month, more Pre-Paid Interest will be due; if it closes toward month's end, the amount due will be less.

| JANUARY | | | | | | |
|---|---|---|---|---|---|---|
| 1 | 2 | 3 | 4 | 5 | 6 | 7 |
| 8 | 9 | 10 | 11 | 12 | 13 | 14 |
| 15 | 16 | 17 | 18 | 19 | 20 | 21 |
| 22 | 23 | 24 | 25 Escrow closes. Seven day's interest collected. | 26 | 27 | 28 |
| 29 | 30 | 31 First billing cycle ends. | | | | |

| FEBRUARY | | | | | | | |
|---|---|---|---|---|---|---|---|
| | | | **1** Second billing cycle begins. | 2 | 3 | 4 | |
| 5 | 6 | 7 | 8 | 9 | 10 | 11 | |
| 12 | 13 | 14 | **15** (No payment due this month.) | 16 | 17 | 18 | |
| 19 | 20 | 21 | 22 | 23 | 24 | 25 | |
| 26 | 27 | **28** Second billing cycle ends. | | | | | |

| March | | | | | | | |
|---|---|---|---|---|---|---|---|
| | | | **1** Third billing cycle begins. | 2 | 3 | 4 | |
| 5 | 6 | 7 | 8 | 9 | 10 | 11 | |
| 12 | 13 | 14 | **15** First mortgage payment due. | 16 | 17 | 18 | |
| 19 | 20 | 21 | 22 | 23 | 24 | 25 | |
| 26 | 27 | 28 | 29 | 30 | **31** Third billing cycle ends. | | |

## Hazard Insurance, Property Taxes, and Mortgage Insurance

All these will be pro-rated and collected at close in exactly the same manner as pre-paid interest; the primary difference will be your choice (or sometimes the lender's requirement) to have these items impounded. Impounding is simply a form of forced savings. Hazard insurance, and mortgage insurance premiums are customarily due annually; and property taxes semi-annually. When they are impounded, the annual amounts of these three items are divided into twelve equal payments, and added to your monthly mortgage payment; and your lender establishes a trust account into which this additional money will be deposited each month. Then, on the actual due dates, the lender will withdraw the accumulated funds and make the required payment on your behalf. In order to ensure that there will be sufficient funds in the account at the time the payments are due, the lender may have to collect a portion of the annual amount at the time of close. (Example: annual hazard insurance premium is $1,200, which is due on January 1$^{st}$. Your loan closes on the last day of June, meaning your first monthly mortgage payment will be due August 15$^{th}$ [interest accrues from July 1$^{st}$ through 30th and is paid in August]. Since the amount that goes into your impound account each month is only one-twelfth of the total due, you will only have deposited $500 by the time the annual premium comes due on January 1$^{st}$. Therefore, in order to have sufficient funds to cover the entire premium, you will have been required to deposit $700 into the impound account at the time the loan closed, back in July [see calendar below].)

| FEBRUARY | MARCH | APRIL | MAY | JUNE | JULY |
|---|---|---|---|---|---|
|  |  |  |  | Loan closes. $700 collected and placed in impound account. | $100 from monthly mortgage payment put into impound |
| AUGUST | SEPTEMBER | OCTOBER | NOVEMBER | DECEMBER | JANUARY |
| $100 from monthly mortgage payment put into impound | $100 from monthly mortgage payment put into impound | $100 from monthly mortgage payment put into impound | $100 from monthly mortgage payment put into impound | $100 from monthly mortgage payment put into impound | $1,200 withdrawn and used to pay annual insurance |

## What Should Stay The Same

If you pre-negotiate all the non-recurring costs, get it all in writing, and lock your rate at the time of application, there should be no changes—other than those stated in the previous section. If you get lazy, it's open season on your wallet.

# Mortgage Brokers Versus "Direct" Lenders

Do not consider a mortgage broker if your *primary* concern is getting the lowest overall cost. In many cases, a broker may be able to make that possible; but he is *not* a lender; he is a middleman (i.e., an agent); and the cost of his services will always be *added* to the cost of arranging the loan. Not all lenders offer special wholesale pricing to brokers, and not all brokers are approved to do business with all lenders who do. Therefore, if the ultimate supplier of the money is providing it at retail cost to the broker, then his service fee will be added to the cost. Since most brokers—like most loan officers—are reluctant reveal what they are charging for their services, they sometimes limit the products they offer to their clients to those offered by lenders with whom they have a wholesale relationship. Unfortunately, the primary reason for using a broker is to avail oneself of an industry expert who will find the best possible deal; and if that person does not have a wholesale relationship with the lender offering it, he may never bring it to your attention. Therefore, in order to make best use of a mortgage broker, consider him as being in the same category as an attorney; he should epitomize the concept of competent, able, experienced and knowledgeable personal service; and if you want or need that, you should be willing to pay extra for it. In an ideal world, a mortgage broker will act as your guide and advocate through a complex, and expensive process, that involves large sums of money and has potential legal implications. He should not only find the best program for your particular situation; but also negotiate the lowest possible rate, and costs on your behalf; deal with any problems that arise during the process; and do whatever is necessary in order to ensure that your loan closes promptly, and without incidence. Should you choose to make use of a broker, remember that Caveat Emptor still applies; and just like any loan officer, a mortgage broker is capable of acting in his own self-interest, at *your* expense. Therefore, you should still put primary emphasis on finding the right person; and do not fail to get everything in writing.

# *When To Refinance*

At my workshops, I am often asked the question of when to refinance; and many people are under the impression that there is some magic formula, or rule-of-thumb that dictates when this should be done. I have often heard that a two-percent reduction in rate is the crucial cut-off point; but the fabled "two-percent" rule falls—along with all related concepts—into the same category as the term "origination fee" (instead of "commission"); and "points" (instead of "percentage of the loan amount"). It is a means of justifying the (sometimes) unjustifiable; it is a myth propagated to increase sales, and does not necessarily benefit the borrower. In reality, it is impossible to assign a single formula or rule-of-thumb to such a decision, because there are so many variables involved in determining whether or not it makes sense, and each borrower has his own unique set. You must answer several specific questions before you may even begin to make the calculations. Here are some of the standard ones:

1. *What is your objective?* Do you want (or need) to reduce your monthly payment; combine two or more loans into one; get additional cash for home improvements, or some other purpose; pay off a balloon note; replace a variable rate loan with a fixed rate; or do you just want to pay less interest? Never consider a refinance without a clear objective in mind; otherwise, you will have no way to know if it benefits you.

2. *How do you plan to pay off the loan?* Do you want to reduce the rate and term and pay it off sooner, or do you plan to pay it as per the contract? How have you paid your mortgages in the past? Do you normally pay more than the required payment, or

do you always pay exactly what is due? The way you plan to pay can make a huge difference in the time it takes to pay off the debt and the total amount of interest you end up paying. Making payments that are larger than required by the contract will effectively *lower* your *existing* interest rate, which means you would need to get a correspondingly lower rate for a refinance to make sense. Here's an example of how this works: A $100,000 loan at a fixed rate of 10%, amortized over 30 years would have a payment of $877.57. If you make one extra payment to the principle per year, the loan will pay off in 21 years. Total interest paid will be $139,644. If we divide the total interest by 21 years we get the annual amount of $6,650. Divide that into the $100,000 loan and you have an effective rate of 6.65%. Therefore, in this example, if your objective is to pay less interest, but you're already paying ahead on your existing loan and plan to continue to do so, you would have to refinance at a rate *below* 6.65% (i.e., 3½ percent below your current rate of 10%) in order to do better than what you're already doing.

3.  *How long do you plan to keep the property?* Will you sell it within a relatively short time, or do you plan to keep it (and the new loan) forever? If your goal is to save money, you cannot calculate your savings until you've recouped the cost of the refinance, considered any increase in the existing balance, and accounted for any extension of the term. For example: If your monthly payment is reduced by a hundred dollars, and your closing costs totaled four thousand, it will take forty payments (more than three years!) just to recoup them. If you increase your loan amount by $4,000 in order to avoid paying the costs out-of-pocket, you must include in your calculations the additional interest that will be paid on that $4,000 over the time it will take to reduce the new loan balance by that amount. All this must then be compared with how much you will pay in interest on

the existing loan, over the time period you expect to keep the property (and the loan). If your goal is something *other* than saving money, a different set of variables will apply.

4.  *How large is your existing loan?* The cost, and the benefits, of a refinance will be directly related to the loan size. For example: the monthly payment on a thirty-year, $200,000 loan is nearly $280 higher at 9.0% than at 7.0%. However, the same rate reduction applied to a $60,000 loan only lowers the payment by about $84. (Both these calculations assume no change in the loan term from the existing loan to the new refinance, a circumstance that could increase or reduce the amount of savings.) Also, the total closing costs will represent a much higher percentage of the smaller loan amount, because many of the costs are not determined by loan size.

5.  *How soon will your existing loan be paid off?* The closer you are to having your existing loan paid off, the more your rate must be reduced, and the lower your closing costs must be, in order to represent a savings. Of course, if your goal is something other than saving money, an entirely different set of considerations must be made.

6.  *Does your existing loan have a prepayment penalty?* If so, you'll need to add that cost to all your calculations.

7.  *How much equity do you have?* Will the new loan allow you to remove existing mortgage insurance (e.g., because your property has increased in value, or you've paid down the original principle balance to the point at which you have more than twenty percent equity), or will it now have to be *added* (e.g., because your property value has dropped, or the new loan amount will be larger)? If it's the latter, any savings resulting from a lower monthly payment may be offset by a new mortgage insurance payment.

All this, and more, must be considered in order to make an informed decision that will be right for your particular circumstances. Yet, in my experience, most borrowers—with the aid and encouragement of a commissioned salesperson—base their decision to refinance almost exclusively on the *rate* they will get. It is almost as if the interest rate one is able to obtain on one's mortgage is some sort of quarry to be pursued and acquired; then displayed, and bragged about—like a trophy—in front of friends, family and co-workers; regardless of the whether the cost justifies the reward. In my opinion, you should remove emotion from your decision and be as objective as possible. Get the advice of a financial advisor, such as a CPA, *before* you expose yourself to mortgage professionals who have a financial stake in whether or not you refinance; and never chase a low rate for its own sake, without consideration for the actual cost of acquiring it.

# *When To Use A*
# *"Zero Points" Loan*

There are three circumstances in which the use of a zero-points, or zero-cost loan may be to your benefit:

1.  Whenever the cash you are required to pay to close the transaction exceeds the amount you have available, or are comfortable paying.

2.  Whenever the points and/or closing costs of the transaction (depending upon whether you get a zero points, or zero cost loan) exceed the additional interest you would pay, at the higher rate, over the period of time you will keep the loan. (For example: you're asking for a $100,000 loan, and you plan to keep it for three years, at which point you will sell your home. Your lender offers you a rate of 7% with two points, or 8% with no points. If you choose the latter, you'll end up paying $1,000 more over the time period you plan to keep the loan [$100,000 x 7% = $7,000 per year, times 3 years = $21,000 + $2,000 {two points} = $23,000. Or $100,000 x 8% = $8,000 per year, times 3 years = $24,000]. In this case, in order to save money, you'd have to sell in less than two years, or choose the 7% rate).

3.  If increasing the loan amount (either to cover closing costs on a refinance, or to reduce the down payment necessary on a purchase) will cause you to exceed the loan-to-value ratio limit of the program you desire, or push you over the "conforming" loan limits and into the "jumbo" category (at which the rates will be higher).

In most any other circumstance, you are better off keeping your costs where you can see them. Also, beware of anyone advertising loans with zero "points" at rates that seem equal to those at which most other lenders do charge points. Despite what you may see on gigantic highway billboards, or hear on high-volume radio spots, or see in full-page newspaper ads; there is no such thing as "wholesale to the public" when it comes to mortgage loans. Remember my axiom: you can choose to have your costs visible or invisible; but you cannot make them go away. Since all residential mortgages are sold, all lenders—"direct" or otherwise—must make their profit at the time of closing; lenders advertising zero "points" loans and claiming to be "wholesale to the public" are no exception to this rule. In most cases, all they are doing is taking advantage of a loophole in the regulations governing advertising of mortgage loans—which state that the term "points" in advertisements refers specifically to an origination fee—and capitalizing on the fact that a borrower who actually applies for a loan is about fifty percent more likely to close with the company to which he has applied than with any other.

Here's an example of how this scam works: You, the borrower, being in the market for a loan, start shopping around for rates. In the course of your shopping, you determine that prevailing rates seem to be hovering right around 7%, and most lenders seem to be charging roughly 1% for an origination fee at that rate. You haven't yet decided with whom to apply, and as you're driving to work one day, you listen to a radio spot advertising fixed rate loans at 7% with zero "points." The urgency and enthusiasm with which the announcer speaks, and the words he says, all seem to indicate that this is a deal which will not last long, and must be acted upon swiftly. You think to yourself that if the ad is true, it is an unbeatable deal; so you call the toll free number the moment you arrive at the office, and set an appointment for the very next day. A couple days after your appointment, you receive your disclosure papers in the mail; and the first thing you do is look at the good faith estimate, where you see that the rate is indeed 7%, and there are no "points" listed under the costs. Satisfied that you've gotten what you were promised, you stash the papers and go about your business for the next couple of weeks while the loan is being processed. Eventually, you receive a call from your loan officer, who reports that your loan has been approved, and asks you to come in to sign the final loan documents; at which point you ask him if anything has changed. He replies that the interest rate is still 7%, and that there are no "points." Satisfied, you set the appointment to sign. At the signing, you sit down in front of a large stack of papers, all of which are covered in fine print. You do your best to understand each one before signing it, and ask questions where appropriate. One of the last things that is presented for your signature is a Truth-In-Lending disclosure, which includes a final accounting of all the loan costs. Since these are the final loan documents, you decide to review each line of the statement to ensure that everything is in order. As you do so, you confirm that the interest rate is indeed 7%, and that there are no "points," but near the bottom of the page is a large sum labeled "funding fee," which you don't remember from your original disclosures. You do a mental calculation and determine that it equals exactly 1% of the loan amount, at which point you protest that you've been charged "points" after all. Here, my friend, is where it all comes home to roost; because your loan officer will calmly explain that "points" refers to an origination fee; and as is clearly evident, this charge is a "funding" fee. Now you must decide to cancel the transaction or to proceed. You consider your options and realize that you would have paid the same had you gone anywhere else; and although it angers you that you allowed yourself to be misled, you decide to proceed in order to avoid the hassle of starting all over again with another lender.

The preceding paragraph is relatively mild illustration of the power of Caveat Emptor. After all, although he thought he had a better deal, at least that borrower ended up with the same deal he could have gotten elsewhere—albeit dealing with a less ethical individual. It is certainly possible that the "funding" fee could have been much more than 1% of the loan, and that many other fees may have been added on top. The lesson here is: pay attention! If it sounds to good to be true, it probably is.

# *Bi-Monthly Payment Programs*

Unless you don't trust yourself to follow a simple savings plan, and you don't mind paying a relatively exorbitant set-up fee and monthly service charge for a lender to do it on your behalf, you should resist any sales pitch urging you to sign up for a bi-monthly mortgage payment plan. Lenders push these programs because they are moneymakers, not because they benefit borrowers (although, that is how they will be presented to you). You need not pay someone to do this for you. You can do it yourself, and benefit from all the savings that the lenders promote, while paying yourself instead of the lender. If you agree to pay a set-up fee of two hundred to four hundred dollars, and a monthly service fee of three to five dollars, here is what the lender will do for you: He will set up a trust account for you and bill you every two weeks for half the amount of your regular monthly payment. Then, on the regular monthly due date established in your original loan documents, he will withdraw funds from the trust account, and make the scheduled payment; and he will pay the *exact* amount specified in your mortgage note. In other words, the amount he pays each month will be no more than *you* would normally pay. However, since there are thirteen four-week periods in a year (52 divided by 4 = 13), your lender will have an amount equal to one regular monthly loan payment left in the account after twelve months. That extra amount will be withdrawn once each year and applied to your principle balance, instead of being used to make a regular monthly payment. By paying in this manner, a loan with a thirty-year term will be paid off from seven to nine years sooner.

Now, is there anything in the aforementioned description of steps that you could *not* do *yourself*, at *no* cost whatsoever? Just divide your monthly payment by twelve, put that much into a savings account every month, and at the end of the year, pull out the funds and apply them to your loan principle. You keep the interest you earn on the savings account.

# *SRP*

A lender, who is also a servicer (i.e., the one to whom you make your monthly mortgage payment), charges a monthly service fee (usually a portion of the monthly interest due) to the *investor* who *owns* the mortgage; in exchange for collecting the monthly payments, distributing the interest to the investor, and administering the loan on his behalf. In other words, some lenders, although they still sell their loans to investors, retain the right to collect the payments and administer the loan on behalf of the investor to whom it is sold; and charge the investor a fee for this service. Furthermore, a lender who is a servicer may choose to sell the right to *service* the loan to *another* lender. The price paid in such a transaction is called a Service Release Premium (SRP). This is an additional source of income for a lender; over and above the origination and lender fees, discount points and overage. As a borrower, if you ever receive notification that your loan has been sold, and that you should begin making payments to a different lender, you can rest assured that your old lender has collected an SRP—even if you just closed the loan with him a month earlier.

# *Notes On Timing*

Most everyone is familiar with the stereotypical high-pressure salesperson, and many people are loathe to deal with *any* salespeople for fear of encountering one of the sharks. If you are one of those people, I am here to tell you that your fears are understandable. However, don't let them overwhelm you into inaction. I have found that most fears are based on lack of knowledge or understanding. The remedy is simple: ask questions, and don't proceed until you are comfortable with the answers. Here's the rule for purchases as well as refinances: When in doubt—wait it out! You will rarely get yourself into trouble by taking your time.

# Part V

## *Special Programs*

The following section is not intended as a comprehensive guide to the programs that will be discussed. Its purpose is to provide the reader with general information that should help him decide when, or whether to use such programs. To the author's knowledge, the information is correct as of the publication date of this book. However, no warranties are made as to the accuracy of any specific features stated herein.

# CalPERS and CalSTRS

The California Public Employees' Retirement System (CalPERS), and the California State Teachers' Retirement System (CalSTRS) both have special home loan programs available for their Members. I have included them in this book because they are excellent examples of mortgage programs that have been established with the *borrower's* interests in mind. Lenders who wish to originate these loans are constrained in many ways that they normally are not. For example: each is required to undergo an approval process, sign a contract with the retirement system, pay an annual fee, submit to annual reviews, and abide by the lending guidelines established by the retirement system for their special home loan programs, which offer Members who use them special features not available to the general public. The features comprise three categories: (1) limitations on the fees lenders may charge, and how they may charge them; (2) off-market interest rate pricing, which is established by the retirement system; and (3) down payment assistance options.

Under the first category, both CalPERS and CalSTRS place pre-set limits on the origination and lender fees, and indirect limits on the third party fees. They also make their wholesale rate sheets available to the Membership via the internet, and require all approved lenders to abide by the rates, discount fees, and overages that they establish. Loan officers are not allowed to increase their commissions by adding to the posted discount points or keeping any overage funds that exceed the amount they are allowed to collect under the pre-set limits for origination and lender fees.

Under the second category, both retirement systems offer, at no cost to the Member, a sixty-day rate guarantee; yet, they still allow the guaranteed rate to be lowered if market rates drop while the loan is still in process—again at no cost to the Member. Since their daily rates are set to be competitive with prevailing short-term rates in the rest of the market, in effect, this creates a subsidy from the retirement system on behalf of the borrowers. For example: assume that prevailing short-term rates (and therefore CalPERS and CalSTRS rates) are at 7.0%. To guarantee that rate for sixty days, a borrower using conventional financing would have to agree to pay from 0.75% (¾ of a point) to 1.0% or more; which would cost $750—$1,000 or more on a $100,000 loan. For Members of CalPERS and CalSTRS who use their respective loan programs, it is free. Also, under standard loan programs, if a borrower decides to lock his rate, and rates fall during his lock period, he must live with the locked rate, or pay discount points to get the lower one. Under the CalPERS and CalSTRS programs, if the market rates are lower than the guaranteed rate on the day the loan is approved, and/or the day the final loan documents are drawn, the Member is given the lower rate—again, at no charge. This creates, in effect, and additional subsidy for discount points. For example: if prevailing rates drop 0.5% (½ percent), a borrower using conventional financing, who has locked his loan, will probably have to pay around 1.5% in discount points to get the lower rate (in addition to having lost his lock fee); which is $1,500 on a $100,000 loan. *Members of CalPERS and CalSTRS get the protection of a lock when rates are rising, while retaining the benefit of a lower rate if the market drops.*

Under the last category, both programs offer Members options of which they may take advantage to obtain funds for a down payment. These options make it possible, under some circumstances, for a Member to finance 100% of the purchase price of the home.

With these programs, CalPERS and CalSTRS have removed much of the worry of Caveat Emptor from the mortgage process for their Members.

More specific information about either program can be found at the following web sites:

CalPERS: http://www.calpers.ca.gov/homeloan

CalSTRS: http://www.calstrs.ca.gov/benefit/homeloan/homeloan.html

Or by phone:

CalPERS: 800-874-7377

CalSTRS (800) 228-5453

# *FHA*

The Federal Housing Administration (FHA) is *not* a lender; it is a government organization that *insures* mortgage loans (i.e., it offers *government* mortgage insurance, as opposed to *private* mortgage insurance [PMI]). It differs from private mortgage insurance companies in the terms under which it will insure mortgage loans.

In order to understand an FHA loan, you must first understand what mortgage insurance is. Private Mortgage Insurance (PMI, or sometimes just MI) is a means of ensuring that a lender will not experience a loss on a given loan in the event of default by the borrower.

"What!" I hear you scream. "I thought that the *property* was the collateral on a mortgage loan!"

Yes, that's correct. Nevertheless, in some cases, proceeds from the foreclosure and sale of a property may not be enough to cover the entire amount due on a given mortgage; in fact, lender-owned (REO) properties rarely sell for more than *eighty-percent* of their actual market value. Therefore, if you want to borrower more than eighty-percent of the purchase price of a property—meaning, you have less than 20% of the price for a down payment, or less than 20% equity in a property you wish to refinance—the lender is going to ask for additional collateral. Mortgage insurance is the way this is accomplished. On an insured loan, the MI company covers any loss the lender may experience in a foreclosure sale.

On a transaction in which there is less than twenty percent equity, the MI company becomes, in effect, an additional lender; and it will require the lender to submit the loan file to its own underwriters for review, *after* the lender has approved it, but *before* it is closed. If the MI company does not agree with the lender's decision that the borrower is creditworthy, it will not agree to insure the loan; which means the lender will probably refuse to lend the money. As a general rule, MI companies are fairly strict and inflexible when it comes to qualifying borrowers; because if too many of the loans they've insured go into default, they will be forced out of business. There are, however, mortgage insurance programs available for borrowers who have less then perfect profiles; and in the same way that poor drivers must pay more for auto insurance, the trade-off is higher MI premiums. One of the most flexible mortgage insurers in the marketplace is the FHA.

The FHA loan program was originally established as a means of helping borrowers, *who could not qualify* for a mortgage under conventional lending guidelines, to buy homes. It is, therefore—by definition—the loan program of last resort. I say this in all seriousness; because although it is relatively easy to qualify for an FHA loan, it will cost you dearly. Therefore, it should never be used if another alternative is available. I will talk about the cost in a moment; but first, let's cover the features of the program itself. They comprise two basic categories: (1) source of down payment/closing funds, and (2) source of qualifying income.

### Source Of Funds

FHA is unique in that it is the only mortgage loan program available that does not require the borrower to have *any* of his own money, yet still allows for an extremely *low* down payment. All other loan programs place restrictions on the source of the down payment and closing funds. Most require that at least *some* of the funds are money that the borrower has saved on his own. Even VA and conventional programs that do not require the borrower to have a down payment, still impose reserve requirements (meaning, the borrower must have remaining cash reserves equivalent to at least two loan payments *after* the loan has closed; and he must prove that he has saved the money *on his own* [as opposed to having received it as a gift, loan, etc.]). Under FHA guidelines, by contrast, the closing funds may come from nearly anywhere (e.g., a gift from a relative, friend or co-worker; gambling winnings; or even a credit card advance!). In addition, there is no requirement under FHA guidelines that the borrower have any money left over after the transaction has closed, which makes it quite easy for almost anyone to buy a home under FHA. However, it also opens the door to abuse of the borrower by the lender, and it will cost considerably more than its alternatives. (See "Pitfalls" below.)

### Source Of Qualifying Income

FHA is unique among loan programs in this aspect also: the guidelines allow for any combination that will provide sufficient income to qualify for the loan, regardless of occupancy. Therefore, it is the only loan program that will allow a non-occupant co-borrower (i.e., one who will sign on the note, but who will *not* occupy the property as his primary residence) to provide *all* the qualifying income on a transaction. For example: under FHA it is possible for a college student, with no job, to purchase a condo next to campus in his own name, and use his *parent's* income to qualify. Another typical scenario is extended families combining their separate incomes to buy a house for one of the group. No other loan programs allows for this type of income combining. Again, this makes it quite easy for just about anyone to buy a home; but it is wise to be aware of the potential hazards. There are five basic categories I have found as follows below.

## Pitfalls

### 1. *Over-encumbering the property*

Since FHA allows certain closing costs to be added to the loan amount (see up-front mortgage insurance below), if the borrower puts just the minimum down payment, it is possible to end up with a loan that is equal to—or even above—the actual value of the home. In addition, it is quite common for FHA borrowers to be relatively cash poor. Therefore, Realtors regularly negotiate a credit from the seller of the property to cover some or all of the closing costs. The caveat is that, often, the trade-off is a higher sales price, possibly one that is even slightly *above* what the market will bear—which only compounds the effect of over-encumbering the property. Even if an FHA borrower is lucky enough to have a tiny bit of equity after closing, it is not likely to be sufficient to allow for a refinance into anything other than another FHA loan, should rates drop (at least, not any time soon). This is particularly relevant if the borrower gets a variable rate, or ends up with an interest rate that is above the prevailing market (see "Discount Points and Overages" below). In all likelihood, the borrower will have to live with whatever he has for quite some time, despite favorable market changes that occur after his loan closes.

### 2. *Up-front, and ongoing mortgage insurance premiums*

Since FHA is not a lender, but rather a mortgage insurer, every FHA loan—by definition—*must* have mortgage insurance; and FHA is one of the *most expensive* types of mortgage insurance available. Borrowers are required to pay an Up-Front Mortgage Insurance Premium (UFMIP) to FHA at the time the loan closes; which will be calculated at more than one percent of the loan amount, and will typically be *added* to the total loan balance at close. Furthermore, FHA charges an *additional* one-half percent (0.5%) premium *annually*, for as long as the loan is outstanding; which makes the total nearly double what private mortgage insurers charge on conventional loans. (And since the UFMIP is added to the loan amount, you will be paying additional interest on top of everything else!) Lastly, the law requires lenders to remove private mortgage insurance upon the request of a borrower who can prove he has twenty percent or more equity in his property. FHA mortgage insurance cannot be removed sooner than five years (and then only if there is sufficient equity in the property), unless the loan is paid off with a conventional refinance.

3.   *Overburdening the borrower with debt*

The main reason that most loan programs do not accept borrowers who have no demonstrated ability to save money, and insufficient qualifying income of their own, is that these borrowers are typically not able to service the debt. In other words, *they shouldn't be borrowing in the first place!* The truth of this matter is evident in the extremely high rates of default under FHA, as compared to all other loan products. Unfortunately, the high commissions that may be earned by Realtors and loan officers on these types of transactions provides an enormous motivation for these individuals to put unqualified people into homes. Furthermore, the additional amounts that can be earned on FHA loans tempt many loan professionals into selling them to borrowers who could easily qualify for less expensive, conventional loan products.

4.   *Liability of co-borrowers*

In my experience, non-occupant co-borrowers are often unaware that they will be directly liable for paying back the loan in the event the primary borrower defaults; which is an extremely important matter in light of the high default rate of FHA loans. Potential co-borrowers must also take into consideration the fact that the resulting liability will show up on their credit reports and count against them should they wish to get additional credit on their own, despite the fact that they are not responsible for the payment. Furthermore, if the primary borrower pays late, or goes into default and loses the home to foreclosure; the credit histories of all co-borrowers will be similarly stained.

## 5. *Discount points and overages*

This is my pet peeve. Nothing makes me more angry than to watch loan officers take advantage of the ignorance of their clients for their own personal gain; and misused discount points coupled with overage pricing on FHA loans is one of the most common, and ignoble ways this is done. Despite (and perhaps because of) mountains of government mandated disclosures relating to this subject, most borrowers have no clue what "discount points" are, or how "overage pricing" affects them. I have found that this is especially true for FHA borrowers, who tend to be naïve and trusting, first-time buyers. Many of them did not believe they could buy a home because of past credit problems, inability to save, or lack of income; and they are so thrilled to find out that they can, they fail to notice that they are being taken to the cleaners in the process. Unfortunately, it seems that those who can *least* afford it are the *most* likely to be victimized. In a typical scenario, the Realtor has convinced the seller to pay two "discount" points on behalf of the borrower, and has written this two percent credit into the purchase contract. If the borrower does not insist that the two points be used to actually discount his rate, an unscrupulous loan officer will charge the *prevailing* rate, and *keep* the "discount" points for himself as additional commission. In some cases, the loan officer may go even further and actually convince the borrowers to accept an interest rate that is *above* the prevailing market, thereby generating an overage which he will also keep for himself. I have witnessed loan officers who regularly collected *five percent* or more in commissions on FHA loans (i.e., the "customary" two discount points paid by the seller [which don't discount anything!], another two points from overage pricing, and the statutory one percent origination fee allowed by FHA.). This is nothing more than outright fraud. Yet, it is allowed to happen every day by virtue of the ignorance, and naiveté of many FHA borrowers, and the lack of oversight on the part of lenders and the FHA.

# *VA*

As a mortgage professional who is himself a veteran, and one who has held two VA mortgages, the author is intimately familiar with this program. That being said, I must warn those readers who are Veterans that there are indeed pitfalls to avoid. In fact, they are nearly identical to those stated above in the section on FHA loans. The worst that one can do is to assume that Uncle Sam has set up this program to protect Veterans from the shark-infested waters of mortgage lending.

There is really only one benefit to using a VA loan: borrowers are able to purchase homes with no money at all. Whether this is a "benefit" depends upon the circumstances of each particular transaction. In my experience—which includes my own two loans—the opportunity to buy Real Estate with "no cash required" often becomes a recipe for financial disaster. In other words, a VA loan can act as a means by which a Veteran can easily get in over his head. Here are the facts:

**Over-encumbering the property**

A VA loan is a true "100%" mortgage. No down payment is required from the borrower, and there is only one loan, which covers the entire purchase price of the property (as opposed to a combination of first and second mortgages). VA goes even further by allowing all but one dollar of the borrower's closing costs to be paid by the *seller* of the property. (Note that the costs don't go away, the VA simply allows the seller to "pay" them.) Unfortunately, these two "benefits" literally guarantee that, at the close of the transaction, the Veteran will owe *more* than the property is worth. There are two reasons for this: First, the VA, like FHA, is a mortgage insurer—not a lender. The difference is that VA charges a "guarantee fee," rather than a mortgage insurance premium.

The first time a Veteran uses this program, the fee will be two percent
of the loan amount, which is added to the loan balance. (If the Veteran
chooses to use this program a second time, the fee is three percent.)
Since the guarantee fee is added to the loan amount, the Veteran will be
paying interest on the fee, in addition to financing from 102% to 103%
of the purchase price of the property. Secondly, it is a rare seller who is
willing to pay all of a buyer's closing costs (in addition to his own!),
without getting *something* in return; and the trade-off is virtually always
a higher sales price. Thus, it is not uncommon for a Veteran buyer, using
a VA loan, to over-encumber an over-priced property.

**Overburdening the borrower with debt**

The VA is a bit more conservative than the FHA as far as qualifying
guidelines are concerned. VA does not allow multiple borrowers to
combine their incomes for qualifying purposes unless the borrowers are
married; or if all borrowers are Veterans, and all intend to occupy the
property as their primary residence. Veteran borrowers must still prove
they have adequate income, and enough cash in reserve after the loan
has closed, to make at least two mortgage payments. As a result, the rate
of default on VA loans is significantly lower than that of FHA loans.
Nonetheless, the qualifying guidelines are still more liberal than
conventional programs; but since the down payment and closing costs
will be financed, the Veteran is generally requesting a larger loan than
would normally be necessary. Finally, since the property, will in all
likelihood, be over-encumbered, should interest rates drop, or the value
of the home fail to appreciate (or perhaps decrease!), the Veteran has no
refinancing options besides another VA loan.

**Discount points and overages**

Everything I stated under this heading in the section on FHA loans
applies equally to VA loans. Realtors nearly always include the
"customary" two "discount points" in the purchase agreement as part of
the closing costs that will be paid by the seller. Yet, again, if the borrower
does not insist that the two points be used to discount his rate, an

unscrupulous loan officer will charge the *prevailing* rate (which is usually already a bit higher than conventional loans), and keep the "discount" as additional commission. And like FHA, there is no oversight by the VA that prohibits loan officers from collecting the "discount" points, and not only failing to offer a discounted rate, but also selling the Veteran borrowers an interest rate that is *above* the prevailing market—which generates an overage that the loan officer will also keep.

Now, lest the reader believe that the author discourages any use of the VA home loan program, allow me to describe the circumstances under which I believe it truly will benefit the Veteran. Aside from the obvious precautions against unscrupulous lenders, there are two things a Veteran can do to ensure that a VA loan will be beneficial to him. First, as with any program, the Veteran buyer should set his sights on a conservative purchase price, one that will leave him with a mortgage payment he can comfortably afford. Second, and most importantly, he should shop very carefully for the home itself, and resist the temptation to buy any property unless he can obtain it for *less* than its current market value. Never bet on anticipated appreciation, as may be the case when the current Real Estate market is hot, and property values are rising; because there is no guarantee that they will continue upward. Even in that circumstance, it is possible to find properties that are priced below market. It will require a good deal more patience and effort, but it will be worth the trouble.

# Sub-Prime

"Sub-Prime" is mortgage industry jargon for a class of loans that are specifically designed for, and directed to borrowers with credit problems. In my personal opinion, this class of loans should be avoided at all costs; because there are very few circumstances in which the benefits outweigh the high fees, and onerous terms involved. Unfortunately, most borrowers who end up accepting these loans, do so because they feel they have no other choice. For a large portion of these borrowers, a sub-prime loan merely acts as a means of delaying the inevitable: foreclosure. Loan officers who specialize in sub-prime lending collect massive commissions (often upwards of ten percent of the loan amount!). The rate will be well above the prevailing market; and the terms will almost always include a variable interest rate, a very short term (i.e., a balloon payment in one to five years), and a large pre-payment penalty if the loan is refinanced. They are rarely used for the purchase of property; and instead, their use is almost exclusively restricted to "cash-out" refinances. The cash is generally used to pay off other delinquent debts (credit cards, installment loans, etc.); or to save a borrower from imminent foreclosure by paying off a mortgage that is in default—including any missed payments and late charges.

The key to making a loan of this type work is equity, and lots of it. A sub-prime lender will never make a loan on a property that cannot be sold for significantly more than the amount he is willing to lend; nor will he fail to approve a borrower who has that amount of equity in his property—regardless of the nature of his credit problems. In other words, sub-prime lenders are not depending upon the borrower to pay back the loan, they are counting on the proceeds of an eventual foreclosure sale. If the borrower never makes a single payment, all the better; when he calculates what is owed to him after the home is auctioned off, the lender will be able to add late penalties and charges to the balance, and collect interest on the whole amount—and there will be plenty of equity available to cover everything.

Considering what was said in the previous paragraph, is there any circumstance in which I would advocate the use of a sub-prime loan? In a word, no. Most borrowers resort to a loan of this sort out of desperation; hoping that, somehow, the loan will give them the time they need to improve their financial situations; but their situations *don't* improve; and the higher loan payments (which during the first years of the loan often escalate) sometimes only make matters worse. In most circumstances, these borrowers would be much better off simply selling their properties and using the profit to remedy their financial woes; rather than pledging their equity to a lender, and paying dearly for it. The problem is that many are emotionally attached to their homes; and often they are unwilling to admit to family, friends, co-workers, and  themselves, that their financial problems are serious, and enduring. I reiterate my advice here: stay away from sub-prime loans. Instead, seek alternatives that were designed to help people with financial problems, rather than profit at their expense. (See *Part V* for information on credit counseling.)

# *About the Author*

Kevin Melody has been in the mortgage industry since 1991. During that time he has worked as a loan originator for three mortgage brokers, three major banks, and one mortgage banker. He spent three years as an Account Executive for the Administrator of the CalPERS Member Home Loan Program, training loan officers, and educating public employee Members; and has been conducting consumer-protection oriented home loan workshops since 1997.

# *Appendix*

Forms

## Commission Agreement

### COMMISSION AGREEMENT (EXAMPLE)

This Agreement (the "Agreement") is made as of this _____ day of _____,
20_____; by and between _____,
(the "Loan Officer"); acting as a representative of _____, (the "Lender");
and _____,
(the "Borrower/s"); and supercedes any and all prior Agreements relating to commissions (the "Origination Fee")
owed by the Borrower/s to the Lender.

I.    Loan Officer and Lender agree to provide and perform all services required in order to originate, process, and close the mortgage loan transaction (the "Loan") referred to in paragraph V below. In exchange for said service, Loan Officer and Lender agree to accept, as payment in full, an Origination Fee in an amount not to exceed _____
    ($_____) or _____ percent (_____%) of the Loan amount.

II.    Loan Officer and Lender further agree that the amount of the aforementioned Origination Fee shall represent the maximum amount owed to Lender and Loan Officer, and paid by Borrower/s, and shall not be *increased* whether payment is made by deducting said amount from the proceeds of the Loan; or from any Overage, or Rebate collected by Lender upon sale of the note, or any portion thereof; or paid directly by Borrower/s. In the event that the Origination Fee is paid from the proceeds of an Overage or Rebate, the total amount of which exceeds the amount of the Origination Fee owed by Borrower/s under the terms of this Agreement, Loan Officer and Lender will credit the excess toward any and all additional costs associated with the Loan; including, but not limited to additional Lender Fees, Third Party Fees, and Recurring costs. If the total amount of said Overage or Rebate exceeds all closing costs associated with the Loan, to which it is allowed to be applied according to applicable program guidelines, said excess shall be refunded directly to Borrower/s.

III.    Should the terms, or the nature, of the Loan be changed after the date of this Agreement, the Agreement shall remain in force as is, and apply to the altered terms of the Loan, until, and unless, all parties agree, in writing, to change the terms of the Agreement herein stated.

IV.    Loan Officer, and Lender agree that Borrower/s will not owe, nor be compelled to pay, any monies specified in this Agreement unless the Loan is successfully closed.

V    Subject Property Address _____

    City, State Zip _____

    Loan Number _____ Amount $_____ Application Date _____

_____    _____

Borrower's Signature                           Date

_____    _____

Borrower's Signature                           Date

_____    _____

Loan Officer's Signature                        Date

Representing    _____

                          Lender

    _____

                          Address

    _____

                          City, State Zip

# HUD-1A

| L. Settlement Charges | | | M. Disbursement to Others | |
|---|---|---|---|---|
| **800. Items Payable In Connection with Loan** | | | 1501. | |
| 801. Loan origination fee        % to | | | | |
| 802. Loan discount        % to | | | 1502. | |
| 803. Appraisal fee to | | | | |
| 804. Credit report to | | | 1503. | |
| 805  Inspection fee to | | | | |
| 806. Mortgage insurance application fee to | | | 1504. | |
| 807. Mortgage broker fee to | | | | |
| 808. | | | 1505. | |
| 809. | | | | |
| 810. | | | 1506. | |
| 811. | | | | |
| **900. Items Required by Lender to be Paid in Advance** | | | 1507. | |
| 901. Interest from        to        @ $        per day | | | | |
| 902. Mortgage insurance premium for        months to | | | 1508. | |
| 903. Hazard insurance premium for        year(s) to | | | 1509. | |
| 904. | | | 1510. | |
| **1000. Reserves Deposited with Lender** | | | | |
| 1001. Hazard insurance        months @ $        per month | | | 1511. | |
| 1002. Mortgage insurance        months @ $        per month | | | | |
| 1003. City property taxes        months @ $        per month | | | 1512. | |
| 1004. County property taxes        months @ $        per month | | | | |
| 1005. Annual assessments        months @ $        per month | | | 1513. | |
| 1006.        months @ $        per month | | | | |
| 1007.        months @ $        per month | | | 1514. | |
| 1008.        months @ $        per month | | | | |
| **1100. Title Charges** | | | 1515. | |
| 1101. Settlement or closing fee to | | | | |
| 1102. Abstract or title search to | | | **1520. TOTAL DISBURSED** (enter on line 1603) | |
| 1103. Title examination to | | | | |
| 1104. Title insurance binder to | | | | |
| 1105. Document preparation to | | | | |
| 1106. Notary fees to | | | | |
| 1107. Attorney's fees to | | | | |
| (includes above item numbers        ) | | | | |
| 1108. Title insurance to | | | | |
| (includes above item numbers        ) | | | | |
| 1109. Lender's coverage        $ | | | | |
| 1110. Owner's coverage        $ | | | | |
| 1111. | | | | |
| 1112. | | | | |
| 1113. | | | | |
| **1200. Government Recording and Transfer Charges** | | | **N.    NET SETTLEMENT** | |
| 1201. Recording fees: | | | | |
| 1202. City/county tax/stamps: | | | 1600. Loan Amount | $ |
| 1203. State tax/stamps: | | | | |
| 1204. | | | 1601. **Plus** Cash/Check from Borrower | $ |
| 1205. | | | | |
| **1300. Additional Settlement Charges** | | | 1602. **Minus** Total Settlement Charges (line 1400) | $ |
| 1301. Survey to | | | | |
| 1302. Pest inspection to | | | 1603. **Minus** Total Disbursements to Others (line 1520) | $ |
| 1303. Architectural/engineering services to | | | | |
| 1304. Building permit to | | | 1604. **Equals** Disbursements to Borrower | $ |
| 1305. | | | (after expiration of any applicable | |
| 1306. | | | rescission period required by law) | |
| 1307. | | | | |
| **1400. Total Settlement Charges** (enter on line 1602) | | | | |

Borrower(s) Signature(s):

X _____

# HUD-1 (pg. 1)

**A. Settlement Statement**

U.S. Department of Housing
and Urban Development

OMB Approval No. 2502-0265

---

**B. Type of Loan**

| | | |
|---|---|---|
| 1. ☐ FHA  2. ☐ FmHA  3. ☐ Conv. Unins. | 6. File Number: | 7. Loan Number: |
| 4. ☐ VA  5. ☐ Conv. Ins. | | 8. Mortgage Insurance Case Number: |

**C. Note:** This form is furnished to give you a statement of actual settlement costs. Amounts paid to and by the settlement agent are shown. Items marked "(p.o.c.)" were paid outside the closing; they are shown here for informational purposes and are not included in the totals.

| D. Name & Address of Borrower: | E. Name & Address of Seller: | F. Name & Address of Lender: |
|---|---|---|
| | | |

| G. Property Location: | H. Settlement Agent: | |
|---|---|---|
| | Place of Settlement: | I. Settlement Date: |

| J. Summary of Borrower's Transaction | | K. Summary of Seller's Transaction | |
|---|---|---|---|
| **100. Gross Amount Due From Borrower** | | **400. Gross Amount Due To Seller** | |
| 101. Contract sales price | | 401. Contract sales price | |
| 102. Personal property | | 402. Personal property | |
| 103. Settlement charges to borrower (line 1400) | | 403. | |
| 104. | | 404. | |
| 105. | | 405. | |
| Adjustments for items paid by seller in advance | | Adjustments for items paid by seller in advance | |
| 106. City/town taxes          to | | 406. City/town taxes          to | |
| 107. County taxes          to | | 407. County taxes          to | |
| 108. Assessments          to | | 408. Assessments          to | |
| 109. | | 409. | |
| 110. | | 410. | |
| 111. | | 411. | |
| 112. | | 412. | |
| **120. Gross Amount Due From Borrower** | | **420. Gross Amount Due To Seller** | |
| **200. Amounts Paid By Or In Behalf Of Borrower** | | **500. Reductions In Amount Due To Seller** | |
| 201. Deposit or earnest money | | 501. Excess deposit (see instructions) | |
| 202. Principal amount of new loan(s) | | 502. Settlement charges to seller (line 1400) | |
| 203. Existing loan(s) taken subject to | | 503. Existing loan(s) taken subject to | |
| 204. | | 504. Payoff of first mortgage loan | |
| 205. | | 505. Payoff of second mortgage loan | |
| 206. | | 506. | |
| 207. | | 507. | |
| 208. | | 508. | |
| 209. | | 509. | |
| Adjustments for items unpaid by seller | | Adjustments for items unpaid by seller | |
| 210. City/town taxes          to | | 510. City/town taxes          to | |
| 211. County taxes          to | | 511. County taxes          to | |
| 212. Assessments          to | | 512. Assessments          to | |
| 213. | | 513. | |
| 214. | | 514. | |
| 215. | | 515. | |
| 216. | | 516. | |
| 217. | | 517. | |
| 218. | | 518. | |
| 219. | | 519. | |
| **220. Total Paid By/For Borrower** | | **520. Total Reduction Amount Due Seller** | |
| **300. Cash At Settlement From/To Borrower** | | **600. Cash At Settlement To/From Seller** | |
| 301. Gross Amount due from borrower (line 120) | | 601. Gross Amount due to seller (line 420) | |
| 302. Less amounts paid by/for borrower (line 220) | ( | 602. Less reductions in amt. due seller (line 520) | ( ) |
| **303. Cash** ☐ From ☐ To Borrower | | **603. Cash** ☐ To ☐ From Seller | |

Section 5 of the Real Estate Settlement Procedures Act (RESPA) requires the following: • HUD must develop a Special Information Booklet to help persons borrowing money to finance the purchase of residential real estate to better understand the nature and costs of real estate settlement services; • Each lender must provide the booklet to all applicants from whom it receives or for whom it prepares a written application to borrow money to finance the purchase of residential real estate, • Lenders must prepare and distribute with the Booklet a Good Faith Estimate of the settlement costs that the borrower is likely to incur in connection with the settlement. These disclosures are manadatory.

Section 4(a) of RESPA mandates that HUD develop and prescribe this standard form to be used at the time of loan settlement to provide full disclosure of all charges imposed upon the borrower and seller. These are third party disclosures that are designed to provide the borrower with pertinent information during the settlement process in order to be a better shopper.

The Public Reporting Burden for this collection of information is estimated to average one hour per response, including the time for reviewing instructions, searching existing data sources, gathering and maintaining the data needed, and completing and reviewing the collection of information.

This agency may not collect this information, and you are not required to complete this form, unless it displays a currently valid OMB control number.

The information requested does not lend itself to confidentiality.

# HUD-1 (pg. 2)

**L. Settlement Charges**

| | | Paid From Borrowers Funds at Settlement | Paid From Seller's Funds at Settlement |
|---|---|---|---|
| **700.** Total Sales/Broker's Commission based on price $ @ % = | | | |
| Division of Commission (line 700) as follows: | | | |
| **701.** $ to | | | |
| **702.** $ to | | | |
| **703.** Commission paid at Settlement | | | |
| **704.** | | | |
| **800. Items Payable In Connection With Loan** | | | |
| **801.** Loan Origination Fee % | | | |
| **802.** Loan Discount % | | | |
| **803.** Appraisal Fee to | | | |
| **804.** Credit Report to | | | |
| **805.** Lender's Inspection Fee | | | |
| **806.** Mortgage Insurance Application Fee to | | | |
| **807.** Assumption Fee | | | |
| **808.** | | | |
| **809.** | | | |
| **810.** | | | |
| **811.** | | | |
| **900. Items Required By Lender To Be Paid In Advance** | | | |
| **901.** Interest from to @$ /day | | | |
| **902.** Mortgage Insurance Premium for months to | | | |
| **903.** Hazard Insurance Premium for years to | | | |
| **904.** years to | | | |
| **905.** | | | |
| **1000. Reserves Deposited With Lender** | | | |
| **1001.** Hazard insurance months@$ per month | | | |
| **1002.** Mortgage insurance months@$ per month | | | |
| **1003.** City property taxes months@$ per month | | | |
| **1004.** County property taxes months@$ per month | | | |
| **1005.** Annual assessments months@$ per month | | | |
| **1006.** months@$ per month | | | |
| **1007.** months@$ per month | | | |
| **1008.** months@$ per month | | | |
| **1100. Title Charges** | | | |
| **1101.** Settlement or closing fee to | | | |
| **1102.** Abstract or title search to | | | |
| **1103.** Title examination to | | | |
| **1104.** Title insurance binder to | | | |
| **1105.** Document preparation to | | | |
| **1106.** Notary fees to | | | |
| **1107.** Attorney's fees to | | | |
| (includes above items numbers: ) | | | |
| **1108.** Title insurance to | | | |
| (includes above items numbers: ) | | | |
| **1109.** Lender's coverage $ | | | |
| **1110.** Owner's coverage $ | | | |
| **1111.** | | | |
| **1112.** | | | |
| **1113.** | | | |
| **1200. Government Recording and Transfer Charges** | | | |
| **1201.** Recording fees: Deed $ ; Mortgage $ ; Releases $ | | | |
| **1202.** City/county tax/stamps: Deed $ ; Mortgage $ | | | |
| **1203.** State tax/stamps: Deed $ ; Mortgage $ | | | |
| **1204.** | | | |
| **1205.** | | | |
| **1300. Additional Settlement Charges** | | | |
| **1301.** Survey to | | | |
| **1302.** Pest inspection to | | | |
| 1303. | | | |
| **1304.** | | | |
| **1305.** | | | |
| **1400. Total Settlement Charges (enter on lines 103, Section J and 502, Section K)** | | | |